When the Apple of
Rotten at the Core

by

Tina Royles MA

As a Police Officer, I knew domestic violence could happen in
any relationship, but I thought it would never happen to me -
I was wrong!

Copyright

Contents

Foreword

Very often on the outside, relationships can look idyllic and healthy. Yet where domestic violence is concerned, you can start to appreciate how some relationships can look this way and yet, like a bad apple, those relationships can be rotten at the core.

Domestic violence is a distressing and terrifying experience; for those suffering from it, it's important that they are offered a lifeline by way of information and support, in order for them to seize an opportunity and take that first step on a journey of change.

As an actress, I receive fan mail from all over the world; sometimes they share the difficulties and traumas they have faced, so it is important that they are aware of other people who have gone through domestic violence too, as well as gaining insight and understanding to get support.

Having met Tina, her passion is clear. She wants to make a difference as far and wide as possible, to help those affected by domestic violence and relationship difficulties. Her knowledge, experience, skills and above all her insight, has continued to make a substantial difference in the arena of domestic violence for over twenty years, and I don't see that changing any time soon. For someone so private, it is a brave step to expose such vulnerabilities, but Tina continues to step outside such comfort zones in order to move things forward to address and combat domestic violence. She is a highly respected professional and a much sought after expert in her field, so to have the chance to take a glimpse into her professional life, as well as the rare opportunity to gain an insight into her personal experiences, will highlight the complexities and also the chaos that goes hand in hand with domestic violence.

Simone Lahbib - Actress

Prologue

When you enter into a relationship that means something, it's exciting and it makes you feel good about yourself, you become immersed into it, and you feel nourished in many ways, because initially the relationship might meet some of your needs and expectations.

In a way, it's like when you see a shiny green or red vibrant apple: if you like apples, it can make you salivate and entice you in to taking a bite and, as you take a bite, it is so refreshing and it's good for you.

When you see a shiny apple amongst other apples, you might spot one or two that are bruised or damaged, so you leave them be. You search for the shiniest and what appears to be the healthiest; the one that you think has the potential to last much longer. Once you have chosen one, you might be proud of your selection or choice, and when you take your bite it might meet your needs and in turn nourishes you.

There are times however when, despite your best efforts to look after that apple, after a few bites you get a bad taste in your mouth, a sourness, a taste of decay and you try to spit it out, though you may have digested some already. You discard the rest of the apple and you are wary the next time you bite into one. They look good on the outside, but you cannot see inside to the core; you are not aware of its journey to you, how careful life has been with that apple, how many times it has been knocked or bruised, in time causing the damage, making it rotten to the core.

Relationships are the same in many ways: when you first meet someone, there is an element of your gut reaction, indicating that a person isn't for you and to stay away, but how many of us listen to that gut reaction, or do we just talk ourselves out of it and give that person a chance? Sometimes it's glaringly obvious that a person is a bad apple and we might steer clear from the offset. Other times it is not clear at all, as appearances can be, and often are, deceptive. From the outside looking in, the individual seems charming and decent; they might have similar values and beliefs to you and you might count your lucky stars that you have at last found a partner who will love and cherish you.

When you are immersed into the relationship, you might start to see the cracks appearing and, as you get to know them more, you begin to see the bruises and the damage. At first, you might feel sorry for them and want to help them through their vulnerabilities. Yet just like the bad apple which is amongst good apples, the good apples cannot make the bad apple healthier and good, instead the bad apple begins to have an effect on the good apple and the impact is then clear to see. If the good apple stays, it too gets bruised and damaged, and in turn begins to decay and finally dies inside.

Growing up, I didn't really think about relationships; why would I, because they might have taken me off course, away from my ambition to be a police officer? That's all I had my heart set on and that meant the world to me. I had casual relationships, but on my part they were not anything serious, because I didn't want them to become serious. If the other person was becoming too intense, I just ended the relationship, so I guess you could say I was ambivalent and perhaps detached from those relationships.

I remember clearly my sister telling me that the way I was at the time with these relationships would come back and bite me in the future, and of course she was right.

Chapter One

Reflection

I never thought it would happen to me; I had a great childhood, a secure and loving family, I had ambition, confidence and self-belief and, above all, I was a police officer.

It can happen to anyone and it happened to me.

My relationship was an abusive one and it almost destroyed me. My aim for this book is to show, literally, that it can happen to anyone, regardless of who you are, what your childhood was like, what education you have had and regardless of any occupation.

I will give you a brief insight into my own personal experience of domestic violence, but much more than that, I want to share with you my professional experiences and knowledge, in order to provide more clarity on what help and support is actually out there for you, or someone you know who is suffering from domestic violence and abuse, or has been in a violent and abusive relationship, and who is still trying to negotiate the long term effects and impact that this complex issue has had, or is still having, on those directly and often indirectly involved.

For years, I would think to myself why me, what have I done to deserve this, have I really been such a bad person that I have brought it on myself? I slipped into this spiral of negativity, thinking I was to blame for everything that went wrong in my life.

Then one day, someone said to me, "Tina if you act like a victim you will always be one".

That really annoyed me I have to say, because my initial reaction was that they were saying I somehow asked for it, that I must have done something, or said something, to provoke or encourage it. I was angry and yet they were only actually saying what I had thought myself for so long. It seemed okay in a weird sort of way for me to think it, because I had lived with that message inside my head, playing it over and over in my mind. For someone else, however, to have verbalised those thoughts, my thoughts, I was annoyed; how dare they, who the hell did they think they were, blaming me?!

It fired me up inside so much that it actually got me to do something about it and to reflect on the way that others perceived me and, more importantly, how I saw myself. I didn't want to be a victim, so why couldn't I stop feeling like one?

Did I act like one, was there something in my makeup or personality that made me more vulnerable, did I let it happen, and where was my mind at? It was clearly something that I needed to explore, to attempt to process and, if at all possible, to be able to rationalise.

Was I alone in my thoughts, did other victims feel the same, or was it that some of us were perhaps more susceptible than others? There was almost a conflict of thoughts going on inside me: the personal thoughts of perhaps I was in some way to blame, because that's what society seemed to also be saying at the time, and yet with my professional head on I knew I wasn't to blame. What was my professional experience telling me, what did I really believe deep down inside, because throughout our lives we are fed so much information from our families, friends, teachers, colleagues, history and our society as a whole, so what were my thoughts? I needed to clear them and work through the fog that had set for so long in my mind and at least try to make some sense out of it; perhaps if I was able to make some kind of sense out of it, I could maybe lay it to rest or by some miracle let it go.

It was like peeling back the layers of an onion, with every layer the tears came and it stung like mad; no matter how I tried to wash away the tears, the pain only went in its own sweet time. I could have stopped the pain continuing by putting the onion away, but something inside was telling me to hold fast and strong, and stay with it and peel back the layers. It was time.

There were times in my life when something difficult happened; my natural response was to run away from the thing that was causing me pain and that always seemed a sensible way to deal with the difficulty. Yes, running away was painful, but the root cause was no longer present and I would busy myself with things, so that I didn't need to think about the difficulties, and after a while the pain subsided. That was how I dealt with things and it seemed to work for me, but the difficulty with it is when that is the only way you know how to cope or deal with things. If you are then faced with a difficulty that you think you cannot run away from, you feel trapped and stuck, then you are left with these vulnerable emotions that you don't know what to do with. You have no idea how to deal with them, because you have never taken the time to look at what you are feeling, what you are thinking. You have never taken the time to soothe your own pain in a comforting and healthy way, therefore you have to look for other ways to cope or deal with those situations, and that can be done in many ways. Unhealthy ones for me were withdrawing from others around me and turning the negativity inwards, and comfort eating.

My partner, Jamie, was constantly saying throughout our relationship that I was useless, I was boring, nobody wanted to hear what I had to say, I was ugly, I looked a mess and if I left nobody else would ever love me because I was unlovable, and in essence I was turning into that person. I was shutting myself off from others that I didn't have to have contact with. Even at work, I would go in and do my duties but not really engage with others apart from the people I directly worked with. If I passed others in a corridor, I would just smile or say hello, nothing more; I wouldn't try to engage in conversation with them and if somehow they had engaged me in a conversation, I felt a sense of panic come over me. There was so much going on inside me that I didn't know what to say without looking stupid, so I probably came over as cagey, cold and uninterested, which deep down wasn't the real me but I had lost the real me.

When I met Jamie, I was pretty slim and did lots of exercise; I also ate quite healthily as well. I wasn't one for sweet things or chocolate and kept myself active, but during our relationship eating became the only thing that I could control, so I would do it to soothe the pain. It only temporarily soothed, because the heavier I got weight-wise, it would bring its own inner demons with it. Eating to soothe the pain seemed to be a message that I had picked up from childhood and also society as a whole; if you fall over as a child, a parent will give you something sweet or perhaps some ice cream and as a child you then start to associate the item of food with soothing the pain, but in fact it doesn't soothe the pain. What it does is distract your mind away from the crying and you focus on opening the packet of sweets, or licking the ice cream, and therefore the space of thinking and focusing on something else stops you thinking about what has happened. Yet the association in your mind is: pain, food, soothing; not great when life throws up all sorts of challenges day to day in which emotions are disturbed and yet most of us don't know how to deal with these emotions.

The same applies within relationships; whether they are generally healthy or unhealthy, there are times when our partners or other loved ones do something or say something that hurts us, or we feel let down or disappointed, so instead of wanting to feel the pain, we look to the things that will soothe that pain as quickly as possible. For me, the food was the soother and the withdrawing was my way of protecting me, it was my barrier or defensive shield.

I knew domestic violence was complex in itself, but I also felt there were complexities within me that I needed to look at, to see if they perhaps played any part whatsoever in the events that happened in my life, or within my relationship. I knew it would be perhaps a long process, utilising all of my professional and personal experience and knowledge to get to an element of the truth, my truth, but it was time.

In order for me to be able to start to explore what had happened, I needed to change my starting position of thinking "why me, why has this happened to me?" to the position of "why not me?" When I changed this position, it helped me begin to look for possible reasons and enabled me to work on myself to get to a position of clarity and to put processes in place for me to limit the odds of it happening again. Yes I was a victim, a victim of domestic violence, a victim of many things and I needed to recognise what had happened within the context that it was set inside. In order to let go and move forward, I needed to process my part in it, because that was the only part that I had control over; once I had done that, I could then let go of the guilt and shame and, above all, the blame.

I was just in the wrong place, at the wrong time, with the wrong person.

Domestic violence is a complex experience and when people are in a domestic violence relationship, there is just so much chaos involved.

Everything is chaotic: the thoughts that you have, the life that you lead, even your personality. Nothing seems to make sense, because you are living from each moment day to day. Operating from an often high state of alert, which to onlookers makes you seem distracted, which is a contradiction because you are always watching and waiting for the next thing to happen. You can be anxious and on edge, therefore appearing stressed or not being able to cope, you might make decisions to meet with family or friends but have to cancel or just not turn up, or if you attend you might make an excuse and leave, so you will seem irrational and perhaps unreliable. This is what domestic violence does, it creates chaos for even the most organised of people. You cannot see or think straight, you don't get the space to do so, so you remain in that chaos. If you leave there is still chaos: the chaos of the practicalities, of the mind and of rebuilding your life.

Even as a police officer dealing with domestic violence, and knowing on the surface what it was and what it entailed and being able to deal with it professionally in my daily working environment, for me living through it every day at home, it too was chaotic.

So why do I think that I'm in a position to write this book, because I am certainly no writer, of which I am sure you will fathom out for yourself?

I have a passion for making a difference and I have gained a wide range of knowledge, experience and insight, not only on a professional level through the different roles which I have been in. I have also been lucky enough to have had opportunities to work with many different people involved in domestic violence, but I also have experience of domestic violence on a personal level.

There is still a lot of stigma and ignorance attached to domestic violence and I want to try to raise the awareness of what it really is like, away from the hype or campaigns, away from the high profile or celebrity cases you might hear about in the media, and show how it is for Jane or Joe Bloggs.

We live in a society where aggression and violence is all around us: we switch on the news and there are traumas and atrocities; at the cinema there is a never ending flow of violent and disturbing films; there is an endless supply of such movies on DVD. We as a society therefore often establish in our own minds what levels of aggression or violence we believe is tolerable or acceptable; whether it is or not is another matter. For example, on a football pitch a footballer might kick, spit or bite an opponent. Some commentators, managers, members of the media and society might say that the behaviour wasn't that bad, almost suggesting in the context that a big deal shouldn't be made of it. People look to justify and regulate certain behaviour in certain circumstances or context.

What this does, in a negative way, is give room for tolerance, discretion and minimising the impact and effect for those involved; however, for those who are on the receiving end of any form of abuse, violence or aggression, it is a traumatic experience. If you are spat at within a relationship, it is disgusting and unacceptable behaviour, but how many victims are likely to come forward if society accepts spitting in other contexts? If society thinks that a bite is nothing or harmless, what message would that send to a victim who has been bitten by their partner?

Yes, as a society we seem to only be shocked by the most graphic of situations, so how does that help a victim have the confidence to come forward and reach out for help? It doesn't.

I want to try to show what domestic violence entails, the subtle forms and the not so subtle forms, and how difficult it is to, first of all, accept that being in such a relationship needs dealing with and then to try to negotiate your way out of. I'll explain the complexities that make it so hard to just leave because of the emotional and psychological forces that keeps you stuck in a place that you don't want to be, as well as, if and when you do leave, how all the turmoil and chaos doesn't just disappear, how the effects and impact can filter through to other areas of your life, but how with the appropriate support and help, and being armed with information and awareness, you can heal and recover from its impact.

For me to do this, I will share some of my own experiences, thoughts and actions from both a personal and professional perspective and hope that you will gain a clearer insight into the issues and complexities of domestic violence. These are just my experiences, thoughts and actions, so it doesn't mean they are right, or that other people have the same experiences or views. It is also clear through my writing how the chaos comes through, because that is how it is for a victim of domestic violence. There is extreme chaos and, when you try to relay it to someone else, it is exactly that – chaos - and that is why others ultimately struggle to understand when it is disclosed to them, because it is hard to follow and to make sense of it.

No matter how hard I try to make the chaos a little more simplified or easier to follow, it still remains in essence all over the place. I cannot change it because that was my life.

I hope you will be able to work your way through the book and bear with the flow of the writing, not just because of the chaos but because I am aware that I predominantly write in a matter of fact way; this is perhaps largely down to the fact I spent sixteen years in the police and things need to be written in a factual manner. In truth, the real 'me' is a reflective and deep individual who always tries to see things from all sides and to explore, if something has happened, what the reasons behind it were. I would say I'm a practical and logical person; other people throughout my life have said that I am, above all, balanced.

For someone like me who is intrigued as to why things happen, and who is also fascinated with how the human mind works, how we behave and how our emotions work, both in a positive and negative way, it was perhaps only natural that my police journey would lead me to specialise in the area of domestic violence.

So, what do I know about domestic violence and does knowing about it and working with it on a daily basis help?

Chapter Two

Merging the Personal and Professional Me

My experience within the area of domestic violence initially came from joining Essex police as a police officer, and very early on in my police career, having to attend numerous incidents which were called 'domestic violence' incidents.

Domestic violence itself isn't a specific criminal offence within its own right, but it is the 'umbrella' word that covers a multitude of criminal offences, ranging from assault right the way through to murder.

Therefore domestic violence can be, and often is, extremely complex. There is no one singular reason why it happens and there are often aggravating factors that play a part, such as alcohol, money worries etc.; however, these are only aggravating factors and are not excuses, despite the fact that many perpetrators try to blame these aggravating factors for their aggressive, abusive and violent behaviour.

I spent sixteen years in the police, with several of those years dealing specifically with domestic violence, first as a domestic violence expert on a response shift, deputising for the Domestic Violence Officer, then moving into the role of Domestic Violence Officer itself, and finally building this workload and area up into forming a domestic violence unit.

As I am sure you will imagine, I have had 'hands on' practical experience dealing with hundreds of victims and perpetrators over the years; this has opened my eyes up not only to the chaos and devastation that individuals can inflict on others, but also to the strength and determination of those that have suffered or are still suffering. Domestic violence has not only been a steep learning curve for me, but it is an issue that continues to give me the passion, drive and commitment to make a difference, raising awareness and educating, and to look at the gaps in services and resources and to try to plug those gaps to help others.

During my time as Domestic Violence Officer, I was given the role of 'Chairperson' of a domestic violence forum, which was a group consisting of partnership agencies, such as the National Health Service, primary care trusts, social services, child protection services, Women's Aid, victim support groups, Local Authority departments (homelessness, careline etc.), through to family and criminal justice solicitors.

I was given this role of heading the Harlow domestic violence forum by the then Chairperson, Inspector Chris Bainbridge

(Retired), who was for me an amazing role model, not only for pioneering work around domestic violence in Harlow, but also pioneering work within Essex police as a whole, creating a solid foundation and platform from a partnership perspective for me to enhance and develop further.

At the domestic violence forum, we were able collectively to look at gaps in service provision and to look at strategies, projects and initiatives to help improve the services for those involved in domestic violence. We held large conferences to increase the awareness of professionals across Essex, to help those affected to receive more sensitive assistance and support. We ran many campaigns to also raise awareness and encourage more victims of domestic violence to come forward.

Whilst the Domestic Violence Officer at Harlow, I was also asked to become a trustee for Harlow & Broxbourne Women's Aid; this was a great step forward for partnership working: the staff, volunteers, director and other trustees were all forward thinking positive individuals and combined they made a massive difference in the lives of many women and children. It also gave me great insight into how hard all those involved in a refuge work, in order to provide a vital service for those affected by domestic violence, during such difficult and traumatic times. It was refreshing to see a clear drive and passion from those involved; it also made me aware of their continued plight of

24

trying to obtain lifesaving funds from local authorities and benefactors. This is a plight clearly faced by all women's refuges even today, plus the limited refuges for male victims of domestic violence. As well as the funding difficulties, I become only too aware of the limited spaces such refuges are able to offer, due to resources and finances; most, if not all, of these refuges are virtually full to capacity. It gave me such beneficial insights and indeed access into an organisation that was historically wary of the police.

Through the domestic violence forum, I also built up strong links with other key agencies within Harlow divisional area, which also gave me good insights into these organisations, helping to build up partnership working and enabling joined up initiatives and projects. Harlow was the divisional headquarters for police stations within the following geographical areas: Harlow, Epping, Ongar, Brentwood, and later Loughton. I was based in the Harlow divisional headquarters, but my role as Domestic Violence Officer covered all of these areas.

During my police career, I also received specialist training and became a sexual offences trained officer, dealing with indecent assaults and rapes, and a family liaison officer dealing with those involved in serious offences, traumatic incidents and murder. Both of these roles were in addition to my main role. Throughout my time within Essex police, I dealt with hundreds of victims of domestic violence, perpetrators who'd inflicted the violence and abuse, their family members and children, and many agencies involved with domestic violence.

When I left the police and moved to Cheshire, I took up the role of Domestic Violence Community Safety Officer within a local authority council, where my remit was to focus on all things around domestic violence. In addition to my role, I became the coordinator for the domestic violence forum in that area and was involved in both the practitioners and strategic groups responsible for implementing key work and policies around domestic violence.

I also was asked to become a director (trustee) for Stockport Women's Aid, which was again an honour and a role that gave me great insight into their fantastic work and the difficulties that they faced on a daily basis.

Whilst working for the council, I decided to embark on training to become a counsellor, and later more specifically training aimed at relationships; I also began work on a voluntary placement with the relationship Counselling organisation, Relate. When I left the council, I became the manager of a voluntary domestic violence prevention programme for Relate. My role was to set up from scratch a domestic violence prevention programme with two arms, one for perpetrators of domestic

26

violence and the other to run alongside it, for the partners of domestic violence perpetrators. Both programmes were based on psycho educational and therapeutic models.

Over the last fifteen years, I have created, designed and delivered training on domestic violence to a wide range of agencies, including a training day for all Essex magistrates, which was the catalyst for their rolling training programme on domestic violence.

I am also a professional speaker on domestic violence and a media contact, commenting on both high profile and celebrity cases for radio, newspapers and magazines, on a local, national and international basis.

As a qualified psychotherapist, I have a private therapy centre which specialises in domestic violence and relationship difficulties.

I don't have any hidden agenda for writing this book, I just want to raise awareness and make a difference; if by reading this book just one person finds the strength to rebuild their life then I will have achieved my aim.

In order for you to gain an insight into my situation, I need to explain and share some of the key messages and experiences that make me who I am, in order for you to form your own opinion as to whether these messages and experiences have played their own part and/or have had any influence on me being a victim of domestic violence.

Chapter Three

Upbringing: Did my fear of loss play its part?

Did my fear of loss keep me in the relationship?

When I look back, now I kind of know just how lucky I was to have had my childhood within a close family unit; I was really lucky to have been brought up in that environment. There are large numbers of children that don't have that experience, they come from broken relationships or their parents may have had a difficult relationship, and they have a whole different experience of life that has then impacted on them.

I had no experience in childhood of relationship difficulties, either because it wasn't around me and I wasn't exposed to it or, if it was, perhaps I didn't see it. If it did exist, it certainly wasn't something that was overt to me.

Looking back at it from a child's perspective, my parents got on really well and my sister and I were brought up by two loving parents. They were married in 1964 and therefore they have been together for what seems like an eternity. My mum's parents (my grandparents) had been married for sixty three years when my

Nan passed away and, looking around at the majority of my relatives, they all appeared to me to be in long term relationships when I was growing up.

As a result, there were no experiences as a child for me to draw on (thank goodness) of anyone around me, in close or extended family, having difficult relationships that I was aware of, so the 'norm', whatever that might be, or the messages I got around relationships, was that people stayed together. People got into relationships and the relationships lasted.

Okay, I recognise now, having had several relationships in my time myself, that there may have been ups and downs in those relationships around me and I perhaps as a child wouldn't have seen that, but the people around me did seem to be predominantly happy and stayed together.

Growing up, I had a great relationship with my sister; obviously there would be little niggles between us, as with any siblings during childhood, but I had a good relationship with her and I still have a great relationship with her and my brother in law.

We were brought up with the beliefs and values to respect others and with the general message of: to do unto others what you would expect to have done to yourself. My mum was always caring and someone who enjoyed helping people; she was hardworking, friendly and sociable. My father was caring and hardworking also; like my mum, he would always make time for us whenever he would get the chance, so I was brought up in a caring environment.

One of the things that particularly stands out for me during my childhood, and has continued throughout my life, was that I was always encouraged to do the things that I wanted to do by both my parents. Both my sister and I were encouraged to have lots of experiences when we were children, we were encouraged to go into groups like the brownies and the guides, and we would have swimming lessons, gymnastics lessons and music lessons. The message that came through loud and clear from both my parents was that the world was my oyster. That was such a positive message to have had, because I for one gained a lot of confidence from it.

Now it may be that my sister and I have different perspectives on our childhood years, because perspectives are based on our own individual experiences through our own individual eyes. It's through our own 'lens' if you like that we are able to view what is going on around us, so if I spoke to my sister now about her perspective, she may well have a completely different experience of childhood to me. My experience was one of a great childhood, one where I was encouraged to do many things and I was supported, loved, cared for and, above all, nurtured.

There were no conversations around 'difficult relationships'. On reflection, I can only remember, kind of vaguely, two times when I might question whether there was ever a hint of a difficulty, firstly one where my father was out in the garden, digging in the vegetable patch and my mum had asked if he wanted something to eat and he'd said no, because my dad has always been someone that if he has started a job, he wants to get it done and will keep going until he has finished (I guess I have inherited that philosophy). Then, at some point later, he was shouted in because dinner was ready, so because he said he didn't want anything to eat, despite the fact it was about to be served up, he stayed outside and continued with his work and as a result mum put his dinner in the bin. I remember that situation felt awkward, as it seemed an odd thing to do at the time, so we can look back at that and ponder whether that could have been perceived to be a difficulty or not. The other occasion was when I was about twelve; I can remember my sister and I heard the front door slamming and we looked out of the window to see mum walking off down the street, we asked dad where she was going and he said not to worry, mum had gone out for a bit and that she would be back soon. It seemed a strange thing to say, as it was unusual for mum to go out ever without saying to us that she was going out. I can remember feeling really anxious for some reason and being unsure of what was going on. Both my sister and I stayed at the window waiting for mum to return, which she did about half an hour later, but for us it seemed like ages, although she had probably only walked to the local shops and back. It was only much later on in our childhood that I brought the event up and asked what had happened. It was that a male colleague at my mum's work had been phoning up for advice over a personal trauma quite a lot and my dad began to question whether this was acceptable, and was asking whether there was somewhere else this individual could get help from. There was a disagreement over the support level, nothing more. Again, we could look at that and ask whether it was a significant argument or issue for them, or maybe not.

I cannot remember any other situations or events we could look at and ask "what was that about?"

It's only by reflecting back that I realise that as a child I was shielded from things like that, shielded from any negative impacts of relationships and their difficulties. There was no awareness for me of anyone in our family going through a difficult time, and I guess now looking back that I was perhaps shielded from many things when I was growing up, in particular around 'loss'.

Loss seems to have played a significant role in my immediate family's life and loss has been life changing for me in many ways in my own life. It was a loss and its effects that meant I left home one day, not returning for over a year, which resulted in me shutting off my emotions from my family and the outside world, erecting an invisible defensive wall or barrier as a way of coping and as a defence mechanism to protect myself from vulnerability.

It was also the thought of not being able to cope with the loss of my relationship that kept me in that violent and abusive relationship for many years.

It was the loss of my identity as a police officer that sent me spiraling into what some would perceive as a breakdown. It was the loss of my 'rock' that would result in me shutting off my emotions from the outside world and re-erecting my invisible defensive wall again, to cope and protect myself from my vulnerability.

Loss wasn't something we talked about during my childhood and yet my parents had experienced a significant amount of it at the start of their married life. First, there was a miscarriage; the next year, there was the birth of their son who died after two days; a year later, there was the birth of their daughter who died after just two hours; and then the following year, there was another miscarriage. Therefore, within the space of the first seven years of their married life, there were two miscarriages and the deaths of two babies; the following year, my dad's mum died, the next year my sister was born, the following year I was born and, a couple of months before I reached the age of one, my dad's father died.

Having not lost a parent, I can only image that the pain and loss is unbearable and so difficult to come to terms with. To lose both parents in such a short space of time, I would think would be your worst nightmare; it would certainly be mine. To suffer a miscarriage must be devastating, to encounter two - how would you keep positive? To experience the joy of a birth and then to suffer that baby's death within a few days - how does someone cope with that? Then, for the same to happen the following year - how could anyone bounce back from such trauma and keep moving forward, willing to try again and again. Also, when it came to my birth, I was born two months prematurely: how much worry and distress must I have caused them too?

I was shielded from any knowledge of my lost siblings as a child, which must have had a massive impact and effect on both of my parents. The way that they dealt with it (or perhaps didn't) was through not talking about it, certainly during my childhood. It was a long time (my middle to late teens) before I was aware that I'd had other siblings that sadly had not made it. That information didn't even come through my parents, but from an auntie that mentioned it in passing. My sister and I then brought up the subject with our parents who said, yes it was actually true, but then it was put to one side and not discussed again with me until I brought up the subject about ten years ago, when I began to do some family research. We were therefore shielded from loss at every possible point when we were growing up and I guess that was the way my parents had to deal with it in order to function and perhaps move forward from it.

There were no direct losses that I experienced in my childhood or early teens except for family pets. Up until I was about four years old, we had a family dog and she had to be put down through illness. I have no real memories of that dog, either because I was too young to remember or I had blocked out the memories to protect myself, because I only have one vivid memory, of us all as a family being in the car and my dad driving us to the vets. The car was then parked outside and I remember our dog being taken inside and then never coming back out and I can vividly remember sobbing my heart out. My parents don't have the same recollection of the event, but sadly that is the memory that has played repeatedly for me in my mind since childhood when I think of that first dog. There are a number of photographs of when I was a small child playing in the garden and that dog was always by my side or in my vicinity, so there must have been such a strong connection that was there and then sadly taken away and broken, so her loss would have had an impact not only on me, but also on our family. So much so that we were not allowed to have another dog until I was eleven. I thought as a child that this was quite selfish of my

36

parents; both my sister and I, but in particular me, would constantly badger them over the years for us to get one.

Having knowledge of all their losses now, I recognise that they were not being selfish at all, they were just protecting their own emotions and ours from being exposed to more turmoil and pain. Reflecting on it with my now adult 'lens', I can see how painful and traumatic the loss of a pet is, having subsequently lost other family dogs and seeing the effect on my parents, in particular my mum's upset, and also through having lost a couple of my own dogs.

The loss of my last dog still leaves a massive black hole for me in my life and even typing these words and thinking about her, the tears are streaming down my face - it's like someone reaching into your body, ripping your heart out with their bare hands and shattering it into a billion minute pieces which are impossible to re-gather and put back together. She was a massive 'rock' in my life and kept me going through some very difficult times; she was my 'lifeline' and my 'saviour' in many ways.

The other significant loss in my life was that of my Nan, who died the day before my eighteenth birthday. She was actually living with us at the time of her death, because the year earlier she had got quite poorly and she was in and out of hospital. It became apparent that she would probably have to spend the rest of what life she had left in hospital. As both of my parents were in the nursing profession, it was agreed that my Nan would come to live with us for her remaining time. She and Granddad had been living in a purpose built annex at one of my aunties, as they had to give up their warden assisted bungalow a few years earlier, due to Nan's increasing lack of mobility and ill health and my granddad's loss of a substantial part of his sight due to glaucoma. Granddad didn't want his wife to remain in hospital and it was agreed that my parents (and myself) would look after her (I was still living at home at the time, but my sister had left after embarking on her own nursing training the previous year), and my aunt and uncle would continue to look after my granddad.

Having been married for such a long time and still being so much in love, it must have been a painful and difficult position for them both to be in. Despite all efforts to ensure regular visits (as we lived 30 miles away from my aunt's), it's not the same as living with each other. Nan lived with us for about six months with a number of trips to, and stays in, the hospital in between.

I loved my Nan so much, it was heartbreaking to watch her deteriorate in front of us. I seemed to grow up quite a lot in those six months. In order for it to be possible for us to have her come to live with us, I readily offered up my room and volunteered to move up into the loft space, as we only had two bedrooms. My dad had floored half of the loft previously for storage, so immediately had to set about rapidly laying boards, so I could sleep up there. I also took my share of the tasks, such as getting Nan up, washing her, getting her dressed and also taking her to the bathroom for all its uses.

Nan was a lovely, thoughtful, kind and generous person, always caring about others, in particular her family. My mum was the youngest of Nan and Granddad's five children and was very poorly throughout most of her childhood; she spent large periods of time in hospital as opposed to school, the hospitals were quite some distance away as they were specialist heart hospitals, therefore Nan spent a significant period of time travelling with Mum to these places, staying with her whenever she was able and allowed, and also my mum spent a lot of time on her own in hospital, so the connection was a strong one between them both.

My Nan was always someone who worried about where we were, for example if my sister and I went to our local shops and she phoned while we were out, she would phone back later to establish that we got back home safely, as she would worry (my mum does the same). It didn't always make sense to me at the time, but again looking back with all the 'losses' experienced and the impact this would have also had on my Nan (and granddad), it makes sense why she perhaps was quite protective of us, and of her own youngest child, my mum.

My mum worked nights within an accident and emergency department at the local hospital (which was immediately across the road from our house). She had taken some nights off to look after Nan but, two days before my eighteenth birthday, another auntie who had visited earlier that day had said she would stay overnight so mum could go to work and both my dad and I could get some sleep; mum was reluctant to go into work, but my aunt insisted that she wanted to help and offered to stay the night, so that's what happened.

In the early hours of the next day, the day before my eighteenth birthday, I woke up suddenly, as if a bolt of lightning had hit me and I had this sick feeling inside; I had a lump in my throat and my heart was beating fast. I felt anxious and I was lying there just thinking and about ten minutes later I heard the scream, it was my auntie's scream.

I shouted down to find out what was the matter, but was told to stay up in the loft. Instinct told me something was happening, or had happened, and it must be my Nan.

There was no way on God's earth that if something was happening, or had happened, to my Nan that I was going to stay in the loft and I didn't care if anyone gave me trouble: I was getting out of that loft, and without any hesitation I climbed down the ladders, just at the same time my dad was coming out of his bedroom, having been woken up too by the scream. Something had happened, it was my Nan, she had died.

The tears began to stream down my face; Nan had gone! My thoughts turned quite quickly away from my own feelings and onto my mum: she was still at work. Oh my god, how were we going to tell her? We needed to let her know immediately; Dad phoned the hospital and spoke to one of my mum's colleagues. He told me to stay in the house; I didn't want to, I wanted to go with him and tell my mum, but he said I needed to stay with Nan and that he needed to tell Mum on his own, and that was the right thing to do. With that, he crossed the road and ran to the hospital to tell my mum in person, to console her and bring her home. I cannot even imagine how my mum must have felt receiving that news, and to have not been there at the time is something that eats away at Mum to this day. She feels guilty despite doing everything possible for her mum, for not being by her side and it is something that compounded her loss even further, hindering the healing process.

I have learnt over the years that it is not only the events that surround the death of a loved one that impacts, but it is the way they are told or find out about the death and how the aftermath is handled by all involved, that can make the difference in the healing process. If this is made even more traumatic than it needs

41

to be through insensitivity, or there is guilt or any unanswered questions, then it can keep the person who suffers the loss in a 'stuck' place unless help and intervention is made.

When my mum and dad returned through the door, it seemed to catapult us all into an emotional roller coaster of events. The auntie that had stayed phoned my uncle and he came over to collect her. My mum phoned my other auntie where my granddad lived and that auntie and uncle decided that they couldn't tell my granddad, who was sleeping, the news on their own, so they decided to drive the 30 miles over to our house and then, whilst my dad stayed with my Nan, both my mum and I travelled back with my auntie and uncle in order for them to wake my granddad and inform him about his wife's passing. My mum also phoned my sister at the nurse's accommodation (about ten miles away from my auntie and uncle's house) to let her know. She was obviously very upset as I was, so in hindsight it wasn't the best way for us to have delivered such news. My sister drove over to where we were and after a short while she drove both mum and me back to our home; my aunt and uncle followed with my granddad, then some of my cousins arrived at ours during the morning to pay their respects.

From the early hours of the morning right through until midday, it was quite surreal. I was brought back into reality though by the fact that I had to leave our house just after midday, to go into school to sit one of my 'A' Level examinations at 2pm. It was in my favourite subject as well, history.

My mum telephoned my head of year teacher to let him know what had happened, as I was so very upset, and he said he would inform the teacher who was supervising the exam, in case I needed to go out of the room at any point. My sister drove me into school and I sat in the examination room feeling ever so tearful and sick inside, not just emotionally sick, but feeling physically sick too.

I'm not sure what I wrote down on the paper, if I wrote anything at all. I just seemed to be staring out of the window for the duration. One of my teachers, who I thought was excellent, came into the exam room as it was his turn to watch over us and I watched as he read the note on the desk at the front of the room, then lifted his head up and searched the room, finally his eyes focusing on me. I switched my stare to the exam paper and alternated between that and staring out of the window.

I was brought back from my thoughts when I felt a hand on my right shoulder and a gentle squeeze; the teacher had been walking up and down the aisles checking on the students and approached me from behind. It was a nice, reassuring gesture and he meant well, but it so very nearly made me break down into floods of tears. I was so trying to hold it together in that room, in front of my fellow students, because that is the supposed done thing, and looking out of the window was a way of trying to distract myself, switching off from my surroundings.

I guess over the years I have learnt to use distraction as a technique to deal with difficult and traumatic situations or experiences. It seemed like an entire age before the examination time was up. Part of me was glad when the time finished and I could leave the room and get some fresh air; the other part of me wasn't looking forward to returning home either. My sister arrived to collect me soon after the exam time finished, to take me back home.

When the results came out some months later, you won't be surprised to learn that I didn't pass my 'A' Level history exam, or indeed that I got a mark of 'unclassified'. It was an early experience of: no matter how hard as a person you try and no matter how much you invest of yourself into something, life can come along and throw you a low-baller at any time and knock you off track, and you can walk away with nothing, apart from the knowledge of life that experience gives you.

The next day was my eighteenth birthday and my mum and dad were trying to make it okay under the circumstances, as your eighteenth is supposed to be special in so many ways. It wasn't and it seemed to set the theme for many a significant birthday year, including my 21st and my 30th, to end in upset and turmoil. Despite their own feelings, my mum and dad had even written a birthday card from and on behalf of Nan. I got upset because it wasn't written in her writing and it would be the last one that I would ever receive. My mum was so upset that she hadn't been able to get Nan to sign it sometime earlier in the week, because she had been so ill, that it just opened the floodgates of tears for all of us.

We went out shopping later that day, because my parents wanted to buy me a gift for my birthday; I didn't mind not having one, but they insisted getting out of the house would be good for us. Off we trundled to a jewellery shop and my mum and dad bought me a necklace with my birth sign on it, and from money that mum and dad said was from my Nan and granddad, I bought another necklace which had a scroll on it with the words:

'God, grant me the serenity to accept the things I cannot change, courage to change the things I can, and the wisdom to know the difference'.

It just sounded appropriate at the time and I loved the words. In the days that followed, Mum had decided that she wanted to go to the funeral parlour and see my Nan to pay her respects. An auntie and a cousin were going too and I was adamant that I was going.

What a strange and unusual experience that was, as it didn't look like my Nan; it made me feel quite numb inside and that numbness seemed to stay with me until the funeral later in the week, when my emotions came to the forefront again. I held out in the crematorium, as I was trying to distract myself by looking at the floor and trying to not let it register in my mind what was going on around me.

It was in the car as we were leaving the crematorium that I got very upset. My dad pulled over and got in the back seat with me; my sister took over the driving. My mum, who was separate to us as she was in the funeral car with her siblings, looked really upset as their car passed us and she saw me so upset. It was then that she vowed that we would all be together at any subsequent funeral.

Other relatives in their cars passed us slowly, to see if we were okay, and my dad was motioning to them to drive off, because he could see that it was making things worse for me. I just wanted everyone to leave me alone and for the ground to just open up.

Over the following six months, my dad dealt with the loss by distracting himself with work, but both Mum and I didn't handle my Nan's death very well (not that I suppose there is a good way to deal with such a loss); Mum dealt with it by being up and then very down, being upset and then angry at herself, and I dealt with it in my way of withdrawing and shutting off.

After a while, I decided that I couldn't deal with the upset and anger, so one day Mum and Dad went out and I packed a bag of clothes and left.

It was as I result of how I felt about the loss of my Nan that I decided right then that I wouldn't let anyone else get close to me in my life, so that I wouldn't be put into a place or position of vulnerability and get hurt to that extent again. That promise that I made to myself on that day has, at a number of times in my life to date, generally worked effectively and the defence mechanisms that I put in place have served me well.

Of course life isn't always that simple or indeed so black and white, as there is such a grey area in the middle and way more than fifty shades of it.

Inevitably, there has been many times, whether unwittingly or wittingly, since then that I have let someone get close enough to me and on such occasions, when I have let that barrier down, I have more often than not been significantly hurt.

Chapter Four

Making a Difference: Why is it so important to me?

Did my passion for wanting to make a difference make me think I could change my partner?

As far back as I can remember, maybe from the age of five years old, but certainly from the age of seven, I knew what I wanted to do in my life and that was to be a police officer. In my childhood, my uncle was in the police and I would hear the stories that he would relay and I suppose that was one element of it, but it was also a message that was installed somewhere in my childhood and from school, in that a police officer was someone that would help others. I can remember reading the Ladybird book on 'The Policeman' (I still have it); a police officer was someone who you could always go to, especially as a young child if you were lost, or something had happened. A police officer was there to make a difference and, in later childhood years, I was influenced by my favourite television show of all time: Cagney and Lacey, which was an American police drama series and I wanted to be just like Christine Cagney, the character played by Sharon Gless, and I wanted to make a difference.

So that's what I wanted to do and I had this plan in my mind, I guess it was a message that I got from my Nan and my parents: always try to do the right thing and make a difference; whatever the right thing might be, who's to say. I would think to myself at quite a young age, as I wanted to sleep safe in my bed at night, then why wouldn't I be the one who should be walking the street and making others safe?

That perhaps strange view to have as a child was picked up by an English teacher in my early years of high school; we had been given a homework assignment and I cannot even remember the exact topic as my school days are in the dim and distant past, but the homework was something on valuing others, putting others first or respect. I can remember writing that if I was walking across the road with an elderly person and if a vehicle was coming towards us and I had the opportunity to push the other person out of the way, then I would rather do that than save myself. It might sound a bit strange, but what I also wrote down was that it would be more important to save the other person because they had built up a history, perhaps would have lots of people in their lives and they would have built up significant experiences and memories and that it was better to save them than myself, because I didn't have, apart from my immediate family, any dependents and hadn't built up lots of memories. An odd thing to write I know; I've always been a person that puts others first, even to the detriment of myself. The English teacher was near to going on maternity leave and the feedback on my homework assignment from the teacher was: "I need to speak to you, can you make arrangements to see me please".

I never did get around to that as she went off on maternity leave and then when she came back it was a year later and I was in another school year; she never followed it up and I never chased her feedback, so I don't know the extent, but she probably wanted to speak about my strange kind of reality or my strange sort of belief system.

I've always wanted to join the police to protect people, including myself. The other reason for me joining was to do with the messages that I had received growing up about having a secure job and for me to have the ability to earn my own money and make my own way in life. There were also the opportunities I thought it would present, such as opening my eyes up to the world. Being brought up in a small village in north Wales, I hadn't really experienced an awful lot around life itself, apart from the family experiences, hobbies and sport - not through want of encouragement, but just that I had never really been exposed to much of it. So becoming a police officer was something that I always wanted to do.

The process to join seemed difficult with several different stages, and then there was the number of 'O' Levels that I needed to

50

obtain to get into the police; I wouldn't have said that I was particularly academic. My sister, on the other hand, was very academic; I was more practical and creative, and interested in having a laugh. So I wouldn't say that I particularly applied myself very well at school, or made the most out of my time there. My ability was average in most things.

This has been reinforced by my mum recently handing me a box full of my old school reports and homework exercise books, from both junior and high school, for me to keep, as mums do. Curiosity got the better of me, so I began to read through some of them and it made for an entertaining read, but it also made me question where that innocent and fun person disappeared to for so long.

My parents were mindful of not building my expectations up too high in my ambitions to join the police. They both would repeatedly say to me to have something else in mind, as I might not be able to get what I needed to get in. They were not saying it to be mean, but yet it did irritate me in a way. My parents encouraged us in many ways and yet this was the most fundamental thing that I wanted to do in my life, something that I'd always wanted to do, and yet I was being hit with negativity.

Looking back on it, it wasn't negativity at all; they were just making me aware of the fact of 'don't put your eggs into just one basket'. I didn't see that at the time, it just made me so determined that I would achieve my dreams and that I would get to the place where I wanted to be.

At sixteen years of age, I wrote off to several police forces enquiring about the cadets, but a number of forces appeared to be phasing them out at the time, so the replies that came back were for me to gain some 'life' experience and then to apply to a regular police force when I became old enough.

My focus therefore became: to obtain the number of 'O' Levels needed, to get my fitness to a good level and to gain some experience that might be relevant to help me get in.

Experiences where responsibility was attached seemed to be a good starting point, so I volunteered with some friends to run the school 'tuck shop' and then volunteered to be a school prefect. In the sixth year, the then headmaster asked a friend and me whether we would be interested in being babysitters for his children; of course it would have been rude to have said no and it would look good on my curriculum vitae I thought, so I jumped at the chance. That would help surely! I also had a number of weekend jobs in my teenage years, several of which were working in residential homes, again bringing a level of responsibility.

When the time came for me to apply to join the regular police force, my local force was not recruiting, so one thought process that I had was to wait until they were and do something else in the meantime. It's not what I wanted to do, but I didn't really explore other avenues at that time.

My parents found me information on the application process to join the nursing profession, which both of them were in, as well as my sister. Reluctantly, I completed the application forms and was lined up with an interview date, but it wasn't something I had ever wanted to do. Yes, I wanted to help others, but not in that way and I thought that if I embarked and got wrapped up in this, then there was a possibility that I could lose sight of my dream to join the police.

I decided to take my future and life path into my own hands and contacted a regional college to enquire about one of their sports courses. I completed an application for a Leisure Management Course and I was notified that I had been successful and could start. I now needed to let my parents know that I'd applied and had been successful, and to therefore put a stop to any nursing training route. They seemed disappointed, but knew it wasn't something I wanted to do and that, if I embarked down that route, it would have been for them and not me.

I started on the course but, although I was interested in sport, I still had firmly in my mind that I was just biding my time and gaining experience. The course itself was more focused on the management of sport and leisure, so included business systems, accountancy, health and fitness. It didn't ignite any spark of passion within me, so I tried to keep myself on the course by focusing on the one element of it that I liked, which was conservation management. The tutor was great and he got us involved in projects like rebuilding a nature reserve, which was amazing.

The second year of college began to loom and my thought process began to change to what I was missing out on by waiting another year to join the police; all I seemed to be doing was delaying it. I began to think that what might be a good option would be for me to apply to any one of the other forces who were recruiting. If successful, I could join a different force, complete the initial two years' probationary period, and then transfer back to my local force. It all seemed to make sense and seemed simple in my mind.

My plan was to apply to other forces, it may seem arrogant but I didn't really care which force or where it was, I just wanted to get into one of them. As it didn't matter which force, my strategy of choosing one was to stick a pin into a map with my eyes closed! Seriously that is what I did. However, the pin landed on the border of the Metropolitan Police Service district and Essex Constabulary district, so I completed the application forms for both. I had never been to Essex before or know anything about it, and I had only once been to London and that was just for the day on a school trip to the National Theatre, to see 'Waiting for Godot', so that didn't really count.

The next part of the process was to be told that I had successfully got through the application form stage. The next stage would be to sit the police entrance examination and, as I was outside both of these police force areas, it was arranged for me to sit the entrance examination at my local force headquarters, which was North Wales police.

This was the part that I feared most; I was already aware of the fact that English and mathematics played a big part in police entrance examinations and maths had never ever been any sort of strong point for me. I could add up, subtract and multiply, but that was my limit, apart from knowing a little trick around working out my nine times table with the use of my fingers.

I did as much preparation work as I could with a limited ability in that area, but nothing really prepared me for when I was sitting in the exam room having opened my paper, staring at the questions. It was then that it hit me that my entire hopes and dreams rested on the entrance exam paper in front of me and a huge cloud of pressure seemed to engulf me.

I can remember sitting there feeling sick, it sent my mind back to the examination room on the day my Nan died. Focus, I thought to myself, don't even go there! My heart was racing so fast and strong that I thought it was going to explode out of my body. My palms of my hands were so clammy, everything began to race around in my head and I knew then that if I didn't calm my mind down and begin to compose myself, then I would lose my chance anyway without even trying to give it justice. I told myself that if I gave my best, honestly and fully, then that was what mattered and to stay in the moment. So I did and answered the questions, all of them, to the best of my ability.

It was a long wait outside the examination room, sitting with around thirty complete strangers, all wanting the same thing. Then a handful of names were called out to go back into the room, I was not one of them. I began to feel sick again, knots in my stomach, my throat got dry and my heart raced; God I so wanted to be a police officer. I'd never even considered in my mind that I would be unsuccessful in my dreams and ambition - that was unthinkable. The group came back out and they were all smiling, one of the others asked if they had been successful and they had.

It could still happen I thought to myself, don't give up, maybe we are being taken through in batches. The remainder of the names were called out bar two to go into the room; I was one of the two left outside.

The second group came back out looking gloomy, so I figured they hadn't been successful. I tried to make sense of what was going on, I thought perhaps the guy sitting next to me was applying outside of this area too, but I didn't want to ask him, he looked as nervous as me. We were then both called in.

The opening line from the male figure of authority standing in front of us was, "So you both want to join the Specials?"

Oh my god I thought. They have got it wrong.

Did I not sit the right examination? Would I need to re-sit it again, or did I fail the 'Regulars' exam but get a sufficient mark to be considered for the 'Specials', or had I in fact failed everything.

I had to say something, but what would I say? I was so shy then, and still am in many environments, but I had to say something! They had made a mistake, a mistake that would affect my life, my plans, my dream, my ambition. No it wasn't right.

"Sir, I haven't applied to be a Special, there must be a mistake," I blurted out.

"You haven't been successful for the Regulars, you're not on my list, I'm afraid," he replied.

My heart sank so quickly; taking pity on me or perhaps not wanting someone to burst out into tears in front of him, he tried to console me by saying, "Why not try again next year, we might be recruiting again?"

"But I wasn't applying here, Sir, I was sitting the exam for another police force," I protested.

He then began to rapidly look through the forms. "That will explain it," he said smiling. It was nothing to smile about I thought; he must have noticed my puzzled look because he immediately tried to explain himself.

The upshot was that I hadn't completed the North Wales police entrance exam, but one for an outside police force, so the forms were branded in a different way. So I wasn't on the list of successful applicants to join North Wales, who had been called in first and were told of their success. Then followed the group that had failed the North Wales entrance exam, so he had just assumed that the two left had been successful for the 'Specials'

58

as the forms were different. He confirmed that yes, I had been successful in passing the entrance exam to join the regulars with another force.

What a relief! Yet what a rollercoaster ride of emotions I went through in such a short space of time, and I knew that wasn't going to be the last anxious and difficult moment, as there were several other stages of the application process that I needed to go through and be successful at.

I left the building, went back to my car and the tears began to trickle down my face and, although I felt numb, I wasn't sure if they were tears of joy or as a result of the buildup of anxiety that I had felt, but one thing I was sure of was that I couldn't stop those tears flowing.

A few weeks later, I received a letter stating officially from both the Metropolitan Police Service and Essex Constabulary that I had successfully passed their entrance examination. The next stage in the process would be a home visit and that meant an officer would come to see me to check out my background and my suitability to progress further. Here's where another issue existed: I had walked out of my 'home', hadn't I!

The 'home visit' was arranged to be done at the place that I was staying; it was a nice place, it was clean and tidy, and my friend who I was staying with was twenty years older than me, so responsible and mature. The question was asked about why I was living at this address as opposed to at my parents, but because I was at college still and where I was staying was fifteen miles closer to the college than my parents, and there were other students on my course who lived in the same area and it meant we could share lifts in to make things cheaper, the officer didn't make anything more out of it. It just seemed like a chat, an informal one at that, just to get to know me a little better. It seemed to go okay, but again I would have to wait to hear back from Essex and the Met to see if I had progressed onto the next stage.

A letter arrived about a month later saying I had been successful on that stage of the process, but I now had to decide which individual force I was going to progress to the next stage with, I was not allowed to progress to interview stage with both, because of time and cost.

My mum had never really wanted me to go to live and work in London. She had been there once before, when she and my dad were 'courting' in the 1960s, and she thought it would be dangerous. Essex Constabulary had always replied back to the stages quicker. The size of numbers of officers within each of the forces differed significantly, so I thought perhaps I would be just another number in the Metropolitan Police, whereas I thought I could make my own mark within Essex Constabulary. So I decided on Essex.

Due to the fact that I was outside of the Essex area, the recruitment department within Essex Constabulary suggested that I attend and have the interview and, if I was successful, I would have a medical on the same day; I would have to also undertake the physical fitness test on the same day as well. In order for them to do this, I would have to wait until the next block of Interview days were scheduled. I had heard about being successful at the home visit stage in the December and had to wait until April for the next interview date. It was a long time to wait when I was so desperate to get in but, if successful, I had the rest of my life in front of me, so I just had to be patient.

My sister and brother in law were getting married in January and I was to be the chief bridesmaid, so that was something to look forward to. They had been seeing each other for a couple of years, so it was exciting times for them, embarking on their future together. My brother in law was in the army, so we didn't know geographically where his career would take them.

I decided it was a time to rebuild bridges and so in the March I moved back to live with my parents. I guess the living apart helped us all in many ways. It helped me take responsibility for my own life and gave me some independence; for my mum, me living elsewhere prepared her for, and perhaps helped her come to terms with, the possibility that I could be moving to Essex if I was successful in the remaining stages.

April was soon upon us and it was time to go down to Essex for 'D Day' (decision day). One way or another, I would know at the end of that day the outcome of my future. I was to travel down the night before by train to Euston, get an underground tube to Liverpool Street station and then an onwards train to Chelmsford in Essex, where the police headquarters was located. I was to stay in the police student training accommodation overnight and then I was to report to the reception desk the following morning at nine o'clock, ready to embark on the day ahead.

Decision day was on a Monday, therefore my train journey down to Essex was to be on a Sunday. Never having been to Essex before, never mind travel on a train to London or experience an underground tube, it was a daunting experience that lay ahead, anxiety coupled with excitement. It never occurred to me or to my parents that travelling on a Sunday would have its own issues also!

My parents came with me to the train station and as I waved goodbye to them on the platform edge, I was on my own with my individual thoughts wondering what lay ahead of me, both short and long term. The journey was great, until I got off at

Euston; the station was so big! It took me ages to work out that I had to go below ground to get the tube. Stupid I realised after, because the clue was in the phrase 'London underground'! The tube in itself was an experience; people including me were like sardines crammed into a tin. My mind was focused on my mum's words: keep hold of your belongings and don't let anyone pick your pockets. I love people-watching at the best of times, but I had real purpose and was vigilant. The train from Liverpool Street to Chelmsford was above ground, so I felt it was a little bit more normal and I just looked out of the train window, soaking up the views. Not as picturesque or scenic as north Wales, but interesting I thought.

When I arrived at the police headquarters training school, I picked my key up from the reception and went up to my room. It was tiny, with a single bed, a sink and a desk. A note on the back of the door told me about eating times at the canteen for evenings and breakfast, but I was too daunted and nervous to go down. From six o'clock that night until eight o'clock the next morning, I stayed in the room, apart from venturing out into the corridor to find the toilets. I didn't sleep a wink that night and I hadn't eaten anything so it wasn't, in hindsight, a great way to embark on D Day, but I just had to give it my best. It worked before and I needed it to work now.

The interviews were first; there were four of us that day having interviews and we were led up to a room to wait. In the room there were coffee and tea making facilities, but none of us touched them, we were all probably so nervous. The interviews were to start at ten o'clock and we would each be called and taken into a separate room, where there would be an interviewer. This interview would take fifteen minutes, then there would be a knock on the door and we would swap rooms. We would have four separate, fifteen minute interviews with different people asking various questions. I was asked things like how I would react or deal with a set of circumstances that unfolded in front of me and what would I do? During each interview, I was also asked about my age and how that would impact or affect me, and what life experiences I'd had. I just stuck to my philosophy of answering honestly - that's all I could do - just to be myself, do my best.

At the end of the four interviews, we were all sent back to the waiting room. We were told that we would each then be called in to a panel interview. This would entail being taken into a main interview room where all four interviewers would be together and ask questions collectively. The first applicant went in; the three of us who remained sat there watching the clock, not moving, not talking, just watching that clock, alone in our thoughts. Fifteen minutes later the applicant came back into the room and the second was called. Again the same process and after he returned, it was my turn. I went into the main interview room, the four interviewers were sitting behind a long desk in a row and I had to sit on a chair in front of them all, where they asked me further questions about my age amongst other things, so I assumed this was an important issue for them. At the end of this interview, I was taken back to the waiting room and the final applicant went in for their session.

When we were all finished and back in the waiting room, buffet sandwiches were brought in and we were told that the interviewers would make their decisions and after lunch we would be called back to be informed whether we were each successful or not. I think I managed to eat two bites out of one quarter piece of a sandwich, but couldn't physically eat any more; the butterflies were going mad inside my stomach.

At one o'clock in the afternoon, we were informed they had made their decisions and we would be taken back in individually, to be told our fate. The first applicant went in and came back out to tell us he had passed that stage; that was his last stage, bar the reference checks so he was excited. The second person went in and came back out disappointed, as he was unsuccessful, but said he would try again and wished us well. I was third in.

The conversation started with that I had travelled a long way to come for the interview and how did I feel it had gone? I said some of the questions were thought provoking and challenging, but that I had tried to be honest and open about my answers. The main interviewer, who was a high ranking officer, said that the thing that stood out the most was my passion for wanting to be a police officer, and for wanting to help others and make a difference and that I should be commended for that. They said that I didn't have as much life experience as the others because of my age, but that if I was successful at all stages then the police way of life would provide me with ample life and work experiences.

I was then told those magic words that I had been waiting to hear for most of my life - that I had been successful at the interview stage! I was congratulated for that but I was told that, unlike the other applicants, I still had the medical stage and physical fitness test to go, so I was to keep my focus on the fitness test. I went back into the waiting room and the final applicant was taken in to learn their news.

I was so excited inside, but still concerned about the medical and fitness test stages, but their words were at the forefront of my mind - stay focused for a while longer. The final applicant came out and had been successful, but had the medical still to do also, so a vehicle was waiting to take us to see the force medical officer, who was at his doctor's practice in Chelmsford.

What a humiliating experience a medical examination was! I'd never had a need to have a medical examination in my life before (apart from when perhaps born as a baby), so nothing really prepares you for it. Needless to say, cold hands and being asked to remove clothing and being examined thoroughly was what it entailed. Ultimately though, the result was no problems, I appeared fit and healthy.

I then was told I could go back and wait in the vehicle until we were both done, and I would then be taken back to the headquarters. By now, time was marching on, it was quarter to three in the afternoon and I still had to have my physical fitness test and then catch all my connecting trains home. We arrived back at the headquarters and I was led to the sports hall, where the police physical fitness instructors were waiting to start the test sessions.

There were about ten other applicants who had completed their other stages at various points, who were also waiting to do their test. I got changed into my gym kit and was assigned a police trainer to monitor my progress and mark me on my results. The tests included things such as running around the outdoor track for a mile, sit ups, press ups, circuit training routines, body mass index testing, etc.; these were all things that I was actually confident about, as I had practiced them over and over again in the run up to this day, and during the test I went for it as I didn't want to be complacent in any way because I wasn't sure if I was graded against the other applicants and whether only so many could be successful.

My dad, prior to his nursing career, was a physical training instructor in the army, so he would have been mortified if I failed at this stage, so I kept pushing myself harder. After the test I was told to go and get changed and then to come back to the office to see them. It was probably the fastest shower and change I had ever had, albeit I was mindful of the fact that I would probably end up sitting next to someone on the train, so needed to smell as sweet as possible.

I had to wait until I was called into the office, where I was told that I had been successful at that stage also and that I had now completed all stages apart from the references stage, which they didn't envisage should pose a problem at all. They congratulated me and said I would hear from the recruitment department within a week or so, confirming my successful progress through these stages. I was then finished at the headquarters and allowed to go on my way. It was now almost four thirty in the afternoon and I had to run with my bag to the train station to catch a train to London and then my train home. I knew I was pushed for time, but as I passed a telephone box on the way to the train station in Chelmsford, I quickly phoned my mum and dad to tell them I had been successful, as they would have been worrying about me all day. They were both over the moon and so excited.

I caught my train at Chelmsford, negotiated the underground tube to get to Euston, but then we were informed that there had been an incident on our route, so our scheduled train would not be leaving from Euston, but that another might be available at Saint Pancras station; what did that mean? On hearing that news, people began to dash in a particular direction out of the station. I had no idea what to do, so I took a gamble and decided to follow them, out of the station they ran and I followed. I assumed all of them knew where they were going, whereas I had no idea, daft really but it paid off, the crowd arrived at Saint Pancras station.

All the departure times were different and it meant that my seat reservation ticket meant for nothing. I tried to telephone my parents from the station, but they were not in. I needed to get a message to them as they were picking me up from the station some thirty miles from our home and I wouldn't be there at the pre-arranged time. I got hold of an uncle who said he would keep trying them and get the message to them, and if not successful he would pick me up. I got on the train armed with a sandwich and a drink of coke; there were no seats available so I had to sit in the corridor by the doors for the whole of my three hour journey back but, despite the uncomfortable seating, I could sit back and relax, eat some food, safe in the knowledge that I was going to be an Essex police officer in the not so distant future.

All my dreams had come true. I felt like the happiest and luckiest person on the planet that day. Yes, the reference part was outstanding, but my referees were my two favourite teachers at school, who both wanted me to go into the police and had already said they would provide positive references. I didn't think for one minute that I needed to dispute that.

I was so happy at that point in my life. Joining the police was what I had always wanted to do; I had kept on with my dream and ambition, not letting anyone deter me, even if they had good intentions. I kept focused and now there were to be exciting times ahead. Anxious perhaps in some ways, vulnerable in others as I knew no one in Essex, all the people in my life were in north Wales and Chester, but for that entire journey the smile was plastered all over my face and I had a warm feeling inside.

When the train arrived in Chester, my mum, dad and sister were on the platform and there were hugs and cheers all round; they went straight out on getting my phone call to buy some gifts by way of congratulations.

A few weeks later, a letter arrived confirming I had been successful at the interview, medical and physical fitness stage, and that I would hear back within the month regarding reference checks.

For the ensuing months, the smile stayed on my face and I could relax and enjoy the time with my family and friends, knowing that I would be separated from them on a permanent basis for quite some time.

Sometime in May, I got a letter informing me that the references had come back okay and that all the stages were complete; and the best news ever was given to me at the point in that I got a starting date to join Essex police in the August.

I had three months to enjoy life with those closest to me. Sadly when one chapter opens, another one closes; in the July my granddad passed away. He had never really recovered from the death of my Nan two years earlier and his health sadly deteriorated.

This, like the loss of my Nan, would leave a big, gaping hole in our family's lives, including mine, and it would be yet another significant painful loss for my parents, in particular my mum, to begin to try to cope with, coupled with the fact that the following month I would also be moving over three hundred miles away to embark on a possibly dangerous career path.

You may wonder why I have felt the need to explain my life up until this point, but although I was predominantly a sensitive and often emotional person, I was also a strong character in many ways, resilient and extremely focused on what I wanted. I hadn't been prepared to stand by and let anyone get in my way and spoil my dream.

So, what went so horribly wrong?

Chapter Five

Victim: It happened to me. It could have been you

As a police officer, should I have been in a better position to deal with the domestic violence in my own personal relationship?

The first time it happened, I thought to myself, "What the hell just happened here." There is nothing that can prepare you for it. You might think, like I did, that if that happened you would do X, Y or Z, but when it happened to me, I did not react in the way I thought I would, I didn't just leave, I didn't end the relationship and I didn't go to the police, 'the police' were my colleagues.

I had never experienced domestic violence during my childhood or adolescent years and, perhaps through naivety or perhaps sheltered from such difficulties in life, I did not even know what the term meant before I joined the police.

Now I know only too well, not only from my own experience, but from the firsthand accounts of hundreds of victims that I have dealt with over the years, dealing with the perpetrators, the children, the extended families and witnessing the trauma and devastation. Not only dealing with the immediate affects, but also the long term emotional and psychological effects.

When I first went to the scene of a domestic violence incident as a twenty year old police officer, it was like walking into the set of a horror movie: things were thrown all over the place, there was mind blowing noise and chaos, there was screaming, blood and fear. Fear of what had happened and the fear on the faces of the victim as to what the police would do, and on top of that I like my colleagues had to deal with and make some sense of it all, or try our best to do so.

Incidents of domestic violence have never ceased to amaze me; the way individuals behave towards a supposed loved one is unbelievable. Why would you hurt the one you supposedly love and why if you have any children would you put them through such turmoil and danger too?

Domestic violence incidents have always been, and still are, complex ones. There is no one clear reason why it happens, there may be many aggravating factors that play a part, such as alcohol, financial pressures, stress, jealousy, fear, but they are aggravating factors not reasons. When we feel vulnerable, we all can react in one way or another, some of us in healthy ways and some of us in unhealthy ways, such as using coping mechanisms like alcohol to numb, or attempt to numb the pain, the hurt or the vulnerability. I have never found anyone yet who sits comfortably with vulnerability.

When domestic violence comes into your own personal life, again it does not matter what knowledge, what experience or what ideas you have about how you would deal or handle it, nothing prepares you for a loved one raising their hand to you in an aggressive or violent manner, nothing prepares you for the barrage of insults and criticisms, nothing prepares you for feeling so small, insignificant and worthless. You cannot prepare yourself for your confidence, self-belief and esteem to be eroded or shattered, and you cannot prepare yourself in advance for your heart not to be metaphorically ripped out and torn apart into shreds.

Nothing can prepare you for the thoughts of "why me, why has this happened to me, what have I done to deserve this, why can I not just leave, I thought this would never happen to me, why can I not stop loving this person who is hurting me, am I not good enough, is it me, can I make things better, what can I do differently? If you are like me and thousands of others who have experienced domestic violence, you will have asked yourself these questions countless times too.

You are constantly looking and searching for ways to make things different, to stop the behaviour. I see it so many times in other people's eyes, the searching for answers, the need and want to understand, the need for clarity and, above all, closure to this inhumane act or behaviour; I was no different.

There is also the belief that we can change our partner's behaviour, if we do something different, or we help them change. Ultimately, we cannot change anyone else's behaviour, we cannot change or control this. They have to do that for themselves.

They can actually change, but only if they are aware of their own actions and behaviours, only if they want to change for the right reasons and are motivated to do so; as opposed to saying they want to change, because they think it will stop their partner from phoning the police and getting them arrested because of their behaviour, or because once they have been arrested, they think it might help to say they are having help for domestic violence or anger issues to lessen the possibility of the punishment or outcome, or they say they will change their behaviour because they want to win their partner back.

These are not the right reasons for change, therefore the chances are it won't happen.

To change, a perpetrator needs to accept that their behaviour is unacceptable. They need to be coming from a position where they don't like the way they behave themselves and they recognise that their behaviour has, or has had, an impact and effect on their partner, children and any others directly and indirectly involved. The perpetrator also needs to recognise that they are solely responsible for their own actions and behaviour. For those of us who are, or who have been, on the receiving end of the violence and abuse, our part is the need for us to recognise that we cannot change their behaviour in any shape or form and we need to understand that we are not to blame for their behaviour.

We victims don't pick up the perpetrator's arm and motion it towards our face with full brute force. We don't telepathically entice the words out of their mouth. We don't open the utensil drawer in the kitchen and pick up an instrument to threaten or use something as a weapon against ourselves, do we? But because we are often told repeatedly that we are to blame for their behaviour, we take this on board and believe that it's true; the reality is that we are not to blame and are not responsible, but yet for most of us to get to that way of thinking, we need to have an awareness and real understanding of what domestic violence is. We need awareness and understanding of the complexities it presents and, in conjunction with seeking awareness and understanding, there is a need to gain an insight into ourselves in order to find healthy coping mechanisms to aid damage limitation of the impact domestic violence has. For some of us this doesn't happen, we carry with us the burden that we are to blame and are responsible, and therefore we begin to question ourselves in every way. We question our judgement, our ability, ourselves as a partner, as a parent, as a friend, as a relative and an employee, and as a human being.

Over time, you perhaps might think that I would have become hardened to it, but you don't deep down, it still can affect you and have an impact on you as a police officer. Yet some people in my life who didn't ever attempt to get to know the real me, or perhaps I never let them in enough to know the difference, sometimes viewed me as being cold and unemotional, which is so far from the truth but, in a way as most officers do, it's as if I had to wear a different mask, or take on a different persona, one that I had to have, in order to deal with the incidents and crimes that I was expected to have to deal with as a police officer.

It doesn't mean that I wasn't struggling inside to comprehend or rationalise the behaviour or devastation that I witnessed. As a police officer, you are just trying to handle difficult situations, to deal with what you find in a professional and practical way and yet need to so often do this in such a sensitive way. It is this sensitivity with some police officers, however, that sadly so often is missing and in turn disappoints, resulting in complaints from the public. You might think that officers who go into such specialist roles, where trauma is so often present, where sensitivity is required as well as the necessity to carry out the job in a thorough and professional manner, would have a heightened awareness, but sometimes this gets overlooked in the quest to tackle the bigger picture.

With officers who specialise in domestic violence, like other specialist roles where trauma is consistently present, they are at a heightened risk of absorbing the impacts of such trauma over time, and as such this can often have an effect physically or emotionally, or both, and might play out through stress and result in periods of absence through sickness.

For me though, work was 'my lifeline.' It was something for me to focus on and for the majority of the time it gave me the ability to detach myself from my own personal life. I loved going to work; it was almost as if it was my escape from my own reality, the reality of being a victim.

I am frequently asked to take part in interviews, or make comments, nowadays for the media on a local, national and international basis, and this is generally from the position of being a professional working in this area, but recently I was asked the question whether, as a police officer, I had been in a better position to deal with the domestic violence in my own personal relationship because of my knowledge, experience and training. I have to say it knocked me off balance.

that what people thought, that it shouldn't or couldn't happen to me because I was a police officer, that in some way I was safe and protected from violence and abuse because I wore a uniform? Or from the fact that because perhaps my work colleagues were also police officers, it would follow that any partner of mine wouldn't inflict any violence or abuse for fear of being found out and for justice to prevail?

Did others around me think that being a police officer made me immune to the insults, the threats, the criticisms, the fear, the consistent walking on eggshells, being in a high state of alert, feeling vulnerable and anxious all of the time that something was about to, or could, kick off at any given moment, regardless of who was around, or the environment that we were in?

Did it prevent Jamie from driving erratically to scare me through fear of other road users reporting careless or reckless driving; did it prevent Jamie from throwing things around and damaging items in the house when my colleagues were expected round socially, or sulking and being moody at social events with my work colleagues, my friends or my family? No it didn't.

I guess that's what the majority really think deep down, that stereotypically domestic violence happens to a certain person, a specific gender, a certain upbringing, a certain educational ability etc., but that's where it goes wrong, because no one is

80

immune to it happening to them and when it does it knocks you for six.

A consistent question that I asked myself, and others have asked me over the years, is why me? Why has it happened to me? It's often this confusion and this difficulty that people have in trying to make sense of or rationalise why it's happened, that seems to keep people stuck and prevents them from recovering a little. Through my own personal experience, and with my professional knowledge and experience, I reached the point of thinking: why not me and that I was in the wrong place, at the wrong time and with the wrong person.

When I say *'wrong place and wrong time'*, for me that meant emotionally. It meant that my barriers were lowered more than usual and I let someone in to get close enough to hurt me; I am not saying that I shouldn't have let someone get close to me and I am not saying that it's my fault that I got hurt, but I am saying that I had never been so exposed on a personal level, intimately as much as this relationship before, and because of this I felt more vulnerable than I have ever been before and I was not as in control of my feelings, thoughts and actions as I might have been with previous partners.

I'd been hurt in some previous relationships before, not in a violent or abusive way, but by lies and affairs, so there were arguments and disagreements around the lies and affairs, but things seemed to me to be a little more transparent in these relationships and I was able to walk away from them, damaged perhaps but not broken. Yes, there were financial and practical issues which resulted from me walking away, and yes there was emotional vulnerability around trust - but domestic violence is something else.

Jamie, like my previous partners, was charming and got on with almost everyone. They had a wide circle of friends and a great social life and, above all, they had a fun element to them. Fun was important for me. They weren't what you would call 'good looking' or sexy, there was nothing about them that would make them stand out from the crowd, apart from being over six foot tall. They weren't motivated by anything and they certainly didn't have any real aspirations in life. They worked because they needed to, to fund their social lifestyle of drinking, holidays and playing sports.

I'd never had the want or need to go out partying when I was in my teens, but I guess I made up for it when I joined the police, because the philosophy of the career is, or was at the time, to work hard and play hard. I had also enjoyed the social life within previous relationships, but this relationship was different, I would feel anxious and became increasingly wary of what was going to happen next. I wasn't really sure if they were joking with their comments or behaviour, or whether they meant it, and I would feel a little uncomfortable, but then I would question my doubts when they said everything was okay, or they reassured me. My judgement had always been rock solid in the past, but it seemed to be letting me down, so I would talk myself out of any negative thoughts.

They didn't have any structure to their life, and certainly no boundaries, whereas for me being a police officer was the most important thing in my life; it was all I ever wanted to do from being a small child, if you cut me in half then, and even now to a great extent, you would see police running through my veins and not just any police force, but Essex Police.

We were therefore like chalk and cheese, but that seemed to work quite well at first. The fact that I was dedicated to my work seemed to create an issue, when I had to stay on late if a rape incident came in, because I was one of a limited number of officers that were rape trained; Jamie would get increasingly annoyed at that. It wasn't something I had much control over at the time, although other officers would be less frequently approached to stay on. I felt I had no choice and would stay at work to deal with such incidents and in turn my partner used to get frustrated and go out frequently to socialise without me.

A down side of working different hours to your partner is that it gives one or both of you scope to have affairs; for me, it never crossed my mind despite some previous partners doing this to me. Gullible you might think at this point, but it didn't cross my mind, and yet that's exactly what happened. Not just once, but several times over and there were signs such as the evasiveness, being distant, the staying out late, the constant attachment to their phone and the money that seemed to be lavished elsewhere. I would question and confront them. In the beginning their reasons for having affairs would be because I wasn't there for them, or that they had made a mistake, and they were sorry, but it would happen over and over again and they would get annoyed at being found out, so they would take their frustration and anger out on me.

First off, they would start by shouting at me and calling me all the names under the sun, saying it was my fault that they had to look to someone else for comfort, love and sex, because I was never around. They felt lonely and that was my fault. Jamie accused me of having sex with my colleagues at work, I predominantly worked with men, so in their mind anything was possible and I could be potentially 'at it' all the time. They felt they had been forced down the route of having affairs because the odds were in their mind that I was doing that too. The fact that I hadn't gone down that route, and wouldn't have, didn't come into it at all.

84

Realistically, it wasn't my fault but I did then think perhaps I might have neglected Jamie, perhaps I didn't show them enough love or attention in the way that they wanted, so therefore they needed that from someone else.

Regardless of what I thought at the time, it didn't stop them from getting more angry and losing it, especially on occasions when they had been found out. They didn't like being found out and to divert things away from that fact they had been having an affair, they would blame me.

On one such occasion when I brought up the possibility of an affair, as well as the insults and the criticisms, Jamie began to throw things around, which was normal for them. We were in the kitchen at the time and they began to throw things at me, nothing that could smash at first, but things like the coasters and placemats which, when thrown with speed, had the potential to hurt if they connected, and connect they did. I was caught between trying to calm the situation down and pacify them and shouting at them to stop because the situation was escalating as normal and I was getting hurt. They opened the cupboard doors and began to throw food in packets and tins at me; some of the tins dented or burst when they hit the floor or walls, so the food splattered; I can remember a tin of chopped tomatoes hitting the wall and being aware of the tomato juice running down the wall.

Trying to calm them down wasn't working, so I tried to diffuse it by picking up the placemats and throwing them back: if it hurt them too, perhaps they would stop, but it didn't. The only option for me was to leave the room. When Jamie reached inside the cupboard for something else, I pushed passed them and went into the hallway; I went to where my car keys sometimes were by the front door in a dish, but they weren't there. They were in my jacket in the bedroom, so I ran up the stairs to get my jacket and keys, but Jamie followed me up the stairs. They were blocking the way out of the bedroom door; I asked them to move but they wouldn't. They were just laughing at me saying how ridiculous I was being, wanting to leave. I tried to push passed them; I'd got out of the kitchen so I knew there was a chance I could get out of the bedroom. I made a break for it and tried to run at Jamie in the attempt to get passed them. All this achieved was to make me a little off balance and they were able to push me into the wall. As I tried to regain my balance, Jamie grabbed my hair, which was about shoulder length at the time, and dragged me to the ground.

My face was pushed into the bedroom carpet and they began to kneel on my back. My right cheek began to sting; the carpet burn that I'd just gained was the least of my worries in hindsight. I felt claustrophobic and began to panic; I began to struggle and move from side to side which knocked Jamie off balance and off of me temporarily. Then a struggle ensued as we were both getting to our feet, I felt a dull pain in my abdomen where Jamie punched

86

me. I had been punched several times in the line of duty as a police officer; unfortunately that is part of the pitfalls of the job. When your partner hits you, it's different; it damages you emotionally. You question love, trust, respect and all the other things that are important to have in a relationship. I didn't want the struggle to continue and my adrenaline began to kick in. I was able to hold them back at arm's length, but then they spat in my face and I lost my concentration, I felt another few blows to my abdomen and side and as I tried to grab Jamie's arms to stop the blows, Jamie's hands lunged towards my neck and began to grasp around my throat. At first Jamie's grip was fairly firm, but then began to get tighter and tighter. Jamie's eyes began to fixate intensely. Jamie was shouting at me that it was my fault, that I was making them angry.

Despite having had police defensive skills training, I was scared. Jamie's hands kept tightening and I was struggling to swallow. My throat was getting dry and I began to choke. I could feel Jamie's thumbs pushing into my Adam's apple. My eyes felt like they were going to bulge out of my eye sockets and they were stinging. I was trying to get the words out for them to stop. I can remember trying to say I was sorry and yes it was my fault, but I don't think any of that was said out loud or in any coherent way, because I was choking. I had no other thoughts, other than that was it, it was over, and upon that realisation I went rigid out of shock. Then I went limp, not only because the energy was draining out of me, but also out of survival instinct, because struggling wasn't helping as it showed I still had fight in me. To this day, it was perhaps my body going limp that changed things, because the slump of my weight going downwards was enough of a jolt to stop Jamie in their tracks.

Jamie seemed to ease me down to the ground gently and began to repeatedly ask if I was okay, panicking as reality set in of what they had just done, knowing that they had gone too far this time.

I just lay there on the ground for what seemed like an eternity, but in truth it was only a matter of moments; the whole incident was over in moments, but it's as if it was freeze-framed in my mind and that each action was in slow motion, and yet a stark reminder of how our lives can change in a second.

Instead of being angry and seeing the situation and behaviour for what it actually was and walking away from that relationship at that time, I felt numb, internally and externally. Jamie began to cry and say sorry. I knew that Jamie had witnessed such behaviour between their parents growing up; Jamie assured me that they didn't want to be the person they were turning into and promised to get help. They were scared of the person they were turning into. They didn't think they could do it on their own, change their behaviour that is; they needed my support to do so.

88

Despite what you think you might do if something like that happens, if it actually happens you are in shock, you are trying to rationalise it, but you cannot. Although feeling numb myself, I actually felt sorry for them because they had witnessed it as a child and because they seemed sorry this time for their behaviour. I wanted to help, that was my nature, so I reassured them that I would support them to change.

For the next few months, things were okay between us; I was showered with affection. Jamie was really trying to make an effort. It was too late in retrospect; I had switched off inside, I was still numb from it all. I had reached a point in my mind of thinking this is how it's going to be. This is how my relationship is going to be, ups and downs. This must be what really happens in relationships, people cheat, people argue, people fight, people make up; the cycle repeats, over time your emotions become numb and you harden to it and eventually you begin to die inside.

Jamie never went to get any help, at least to my knowledge. My life changed from that point onwards, I never wanted to be in that situation again so I would try to pacify Jamie at all costs, even to the detriment of my own health emotionally and physically, but I began to withdraw into myself and become more isolated from friends and family. Not only through fear that something would happen, but through the embarrassment and shame and of not wanting anyone to find out that it was happening to me. I would go out of my way to cover all tracks of any future bad behaviour where possible and, because I was always on edge anxious with what might happen, I was often the one that other people, including friends and family, thought was being difficult, or having mood swings, or being quiet or distant. It often seemed like I couldn't win, whatever I said or did, conflict would be present.

Conflict was in my relationship and I faced potential conflict everyday as a police officer. Conflict could occur anywhere. It had been around whilst I was a child at school too. It was the kind of school playground stuff which did not really directly involve me, but the result did in a way. On one occasion at school, just after the morning break, we were all in the playground and we had to line up in our classes in the yard before walking back into class; whilst lining up, I banged into another child's arm by mistake and in retaliation the boy shoved me with such force that I fell to the ground and grazed my knee, which began to bleed. My friends came to my aid and we got back into line and then returned to our classes.

As a child, I found it easy to be friends with both the girls and the boys, and I was the only girl in the school who the boys allowed to play with them at play times, games such as tag and even games which the boys considered their serious sports, such as football. In the latter years, I was allowed to play cricket with them too.

Therefore, when the news circulated around the classes that I had been shoved to the ground, not circulated through me I would like to point out, the other boys were not happy. Towards the end of the day, I got wind of the fact that it had been arranged that a fight was on after school, just outside the school gates on the bridge between some of the boys and the boy that shoved me. I told the other boys not to get involved but they were not happy with what had happened.

At the end of school, everyone began piling out of their classes and heading to the bridge. I waited for my sister who was in the year above me at the same school, because we walked home together with two other friends; I told them what was about to happen on the bridge, we decided to not get involved in it and walked home.

The next day, at the end of morning assembly, the principal told us all that there had been a fight outside the school and that all those involved and responsible would be punished as this sort of behaviour was not acceptable. The boy who shoved me had his name read out and he was told to go to the principal's office straight away. Four other boys' names were read out and my name too; we also had to go straight to the principal's office. My first reaction, even though I was only about nine at the time, was that I must have been asked to attend to explain the initial incident, i.e. my fall in the playground line up. Regardless of the purpose, I felt a great sense of shame and embarrassment that my name was read out in the assembly, as I never intentionally strayed from being good; mischievous perhaps, but I never misbehaved.

When we got into the principal's office, all six of us were asked to line up with our right hands outstretched; my heart fell into my mouth, I had a sick feeling in my stomach. Oh my god, this cannot be happening, I thought, but it was. The principal was going to give us all the cane and did not seem to give anyone there the opportunity to explain themselves. The principal picked up the wooden cane, which was a thin long piece of wood rounded in shape, stood by the first boy whose arm and hand was outstretched and brought the cane down onto his palm, the boy screamed and began to cry. The principal then moved along to the next boy and the same again happened. I was at the end of the line, so I could see and hear the impact and effect and my heart was beating so fast I thought it would explode at any point.

I felt agitated and scared. I was also really upset that I was standing in the line, because I had not done anything. I was going to be punished for someone else's actions. It was about me, but not because of me if that makes sense.

92

The principal moved to me next and one of the boys who had already been caned shouted out, "Please stop, she didn't do anything!" It was then that the other three boys said the same.

The principal must have thought they were saying that because they were my friends, so asked me a couple of questions, "Did you know a fight was planned because of you?"

What could I say apart from the truth, so I replied, "Yes, I did!"

"So what part did you play in the fight," the principal asked.

"None, I just walked away," I nervously replied.

The principal asked the boy who had shoved me if that was correct and the boy confirmed it was. The principal told me that I was lucky and that I could leave the office and go back to class.

As I closed the office door behind me, I leant up against the wall outside in the corridor and took a deep sigh. Yes I was lucky because the principal did not hit me with the cane, but I was upset because I should not have been in there in the first place. What was notable though was that the boys intervened, they were in pain themselves but their thoughts were of me? It was a conflicting message that I took from that situation: do you walk away and not get involved with a possibility of still getting accused of something, or do you stay and fight because you are going to get blamed for it anyway.

I had always been led to believe that telling the truth was the right thing to do no matter what, but I hadn't been given the opportunity to tell the truth and it was only because of that one boy stepping up above the parapet that I came out of that situation physically unscathed, although emotionally it had impacted on me.

It embedded a message in me that I have continued with throughout my life, moving forward to put my head above the parapet too, when I could see a possible injustice happening. This course of action hasn't always served me well, and has personally caused me a great deal of angst and sleepless nights over the years, but it always leads me to the decision to do the 'right' thing, whatever that 'right' thing might be who can say, when other people are being penalised or in danger. Somehow though, I never really used to use the same logic or approach when the situation involved me.

Conflict also arose a few weeks after the above incident, where a relative of the boy who shoved me followed my sister, two friends and me, on our route home across a field. At one point, this relative jumped on my back and we both fell to the ground. Then the person tried to hit me; my sister immediately reacted and pulled them off me and told them to get lost. As for me though, I did not react as I did not want to get in trouble with the school again, so I just let them jump on my back. I thought, do your worst and then leave me alone. My sister did not react the same as me, she intervened, but I did not want any chance or possibility of further trouble coming my way, from this family or the school.

Again, the lesson that I learnt from this was that when the conflict involved me in some way personally, I should take a step back and let them do their worst and when they are finished they will perhaps leave me alone, or go away until the next time and I would deal with the consequences.

The next time something came my way was when I was about fourteen, when I was on the school bus on the way home from high school. It was our stop to get off; my sister and I and one or two others getting off were on the top deck of the double-decker. I was the last one to go down the stairs and as I began someone from upstairs shouted, "Ginger nut!" at me (when I was younger I had very red/ginger natural hair) and as I looked back up the stairs someone's spit landed on my forehead, and started to run down into my eye. I can remember getting off the bus and crying, not only because it was disgusting (still to this day I hate it when someone spits at me, it's occurred once or twice in my police career whilst apprehending someone and also in my relationship), but why would someone do that to me? I had not done anything to them. I didn't even know who it was that did it; I only knew that they did it because they thought they could. I was a target just because I was different or more vulnerable.

Until that point in my life, I had never really thought about my appearance or how I presented myself and I had always been really confident, full of mischief, the practical joker with all my friends and with my family, and I was confident enough to play sport with the boys and get involved.

Being called 'Ginger nut' and the action that followed made me more conscious of my appearance, and that feeling of shame and being different. I did not want to put myself forward where I could be singled out and ridiculed, so I became mindful of what I put myself forward for and engaged in.

A dilemma that emerged was of the importance for me to move forward and do the things that I wanted to do in my life, and yet of not wanting to put myself forward for fear of ridicule.

It was this fear of being ridiculed that surfaced again during my police training, standing up in front of the class giving a presentation around a definition of a particular crime as part of a group. It wasn't my turn to speak but I felt nervous. When I get nervous, suddenly my arms become an issue and I don't know

96

what to do with them. I've learnt over the years and many presentations later, to link my hands together in front of me, which now seems to ease some of my nerves, but back then I crossed my arms, not folding them but one over the other. When it came to my turn to speak, my voice was shaky and a little on the quiet side. I had to write on the flip chart paper as well, when part of the session became interactive with feedback, so I stood close to the flip chart, listening and writing down what others were saying.

Why this situation stands out for me, and why I'm telling you this now, is because it has unfortunately played repeatedly in my mind throughout the years and impedes my ability to grow and develop. It doesn't always stop me doing things that I'm uncomfortable with or are outside of my comfort zone, but back then it affected me greatly. The tutors noted down and recorded in a formal assessment, citing through my body language during this presentation, that I was timid, weak, lacking of any drive or motivation, was not up to dealing with challenges and that, in their opinion, I would never manage as a police officer out on the street, dealing with any member of the public, let alone criminals.

Rather than speak to me after the presentation to find out what was going on for me, they assumed and put their own take on it and wrote it down several weeks later when it came to completing the assessment.

This just reinforced my lack of confidence within a group environment and opened me up to being more sensitive and conscious of what other people think or feel about me, including feeling uncomfortable with expressing my opinions or having my voice heard in such an environment.

It still to this day takes a lot for me in a group environment to speak or enter into a discussion, for fear of looking stupid and being ridiculed. The only time I actually feel comfortable with engaging is when I'm in a meeting, I'm delivering training, or facilitating group work that's on the subject of domestic violence; I have worked in this field for such a long time, I have a wide range of knowledge and experience, both on a professional and personal basis, therefore it makes me feel that I'm on a stronger footing, can hold my own and in turn it gives me more confidence to speak and share information.

When it comes to talking about me however, or anything else that I'm not confident about, then I still struggle big time, especially when I step outside my comfort zone, or with people I don't know in a small group environment. I muster up the courage to speak and then someone challenges or queries what I have said and the confidence immediately goes. My words begin to stumble and the nerves take over; I must look and sound like a complete fool. Then I feel that I have everyone's eyes on me and I feel even more vulnerable. This is a continual struggle for me, one that I'm always trying to conquer and, hopefully one day, I will, but it just shows how messages fed to us or imposed onto us, can have long term or lasting effects and impede our development or have an effect on our emotional wellbeing.

It is this feeling of people judging me or me being ridiculed that made me feel more exposed when Jamie made or created a scene in public. We could be walking around a shop and if I didn't answer them quick enough or I wasn't paying them what they deemed to be sufficient attention, then the insults would start flying, or they would storm out of the shop. I was always trying to be one step ahead, trying to assess and monitoring their behaviour to prevent things happening. This wasn't always achievable though; although some of Jamie's behaviour was predictable, based on previous incidents and the warning signs from the patterns which emerged or similar chain of events, Jamie could also be extremely unpredictable in other ways. I hated scenes and Jamie knew that, I just wanted the ground to open up and for me to be able to disappear. There was a constant need to be on edge and that high state of anxiety and alertness takes its toll.

On one occasion, we were both in the kitchen cooking dinner and I was busy chopping some mushrooms; as I was focused and in my own world, I didn't hear Jamie tell me to pass the spices, so I didn't. Apparently, Jamie asked me again also and because I didn't respond, they turned around and lashed out with what was in their hand at the time. What was bizarre for me is that I didn't hear Jamie asking me to pass anything the first or second time, it is only by them relaying that after the fact that they told me they were frustrated by me not answering them. The first thing I knew about anything was feeling a thump on my upper arm and a piercing sting.

I'd felt a similar piercing sting years earlier through my work, when a female offender bit my upper arm; the offender, who I later learnt had downed a whole bottle of vodka and smoked several joints that day, bit into my arm so deep she actually managed to close her teeth together after entry into my skin, she was probably so high on drink and drugs she had the strength and adrenaline to do that. She wouldn't release her grip at all, despite several release techniques being applied by me and a number of my colleagues. One bright spark, however, thought they would pull my arm away from this offender's grip and I watched, almost in slow motion, as a piece of my skin the size of a Cadbury's cream egg, shaped like a rugby ball, lifted away from the rest of my arm and was only left attached by a thin strip of skin where her teeth had clenched. It was a clean cut with limited blood, but the pain was such a piercing and searing pain that it brought tears to my eyes. I went straight to the hospital

100

but, because of such a long wait to get seen, infection set in and I had three courses of antibiotics to clear it up, plus I had to have an HIV test and wait a few months for the results to come back. That came with the territory in the police.

However, in the kitchen with my partner, the same searing pain came over me, Jamie had punched me whilst holding the fork that they had in their hand and the four prongs had penetrated my skin, again a clean cut with limited blood because the fork had come out as quick as it had gone in. I was shocked, what was that all about, I wasn't polite in my response and I literally said, 'What the f... was that about?" and "Don't ignore me then," came the response.

Seriously, me not hearing them warranted that reaction? I just walked out of the kitchen into the dining room and just sat down on a chair. I couldn't believe what had happened. Every time something happened, there was a sense of disbelief that came over me, but again the tears began to flow. "You need to phone your station and get me arrested, I know I shouldn't have done that," Jamie begged.

Was I really likely to get my colleagues involved? Jamie knew deep down I wouldn't do that, because that issue was wrapped up in its own difficulties for me. Nowadays, I wouldn't have any hesitation in phoning the police if someone raised a hand to me, because I am strong enough in myself and I respect myself enough now to not let anyone do that to me again, but back then I wasn't strong enough to admit to my colleagues what was happening or what had just happened. That evening, I asked Jamie to just leave me alone. I put a dressing on the wound and sat all evening in the dining room, whilst Jamie watched television in the lounge. Every now and again, Jamie would come in to see me and ask if I was okay. My responses were cold and they would sheepishly leave, or come back in with a glass of wine as a peace offering. I wasn't in any kind of mood for a truce. I just continued to shut myself off both externally and internally.

I was reluctant to take annual leave from work and it would always get to a point when one of my bosses would usually suggest that I needed to take the time off, as I had too many days left; reluctantly I took time off therefore. Some holidays when Jamie and I spent time together would go relatively smoothly, and yet there were other times when I would spend the majority of the holiday on my own, because Jamie was either sulking over something that had happened, or they had stormed off because of me or someone else, it never mattered what. I would be left not knowing what mood they would be in when they returned. It wouldn't matter where we were on holiday and it didn't seem to make any difference if we were on holiday on our own or with friends or family. A flare up could happen over what might seem nothing and escalate into a big scene that could last hours or days and I would be left to pick up the pieces or to deal with the consequences, or the questions from friends or family, or the knowing glances.

There were many occasions that were ruined by Jamie's behaviour. It didn't always need to be overt behaviour, it could also be subtle behaviour, the words whispered into my ear that onlookers might have thought were sweet nothings and romantic, but they were not sweet nothings. If I just so happened to glance over in someone's direction for a second too long when we were out, then I was "wanting to have an affair with someone." In truth, if I looked over in someone else's direction, it would be that I was trying to take a glimpse into someone else's life, wishing it was mine. Of course I didn't know, or wouldn't have been able to tell, whether that someone else's life was any better than mine, I just assumed it would be.

One occasion, we came back from being at friends and a row ensued as I had apparently spent too much time talking to one of our friends. Jamie slapped me across the face. Feeling brave, I said I wasn't in the mood to deal with such crap, so I went upstairs and lay on the bed. Jamie came up after me; I was face down on the bed and they straddled me and punched so hard with what was only a clenched fist, but it connected and I felt a searing pain; I just spent the afternoon crying into the bed sheets.

A few days later, I went to the doctor about the pain. My doctor also knew me in a professional capacity so, if push came to shove, I would have said it happened at work, but she inadvertently made that easier for me by asking if it had happened at work. I gave her a look that could have been taken as a 'yes' or a 'no', but she seemed to settle on the 'yes'. The upshot of my visit though was that there was inflammation and damage and it would take several weeks to heal. I did come clean to my doctor at one point in the future when I felt strong enough, and from then onwards, she was someone who helped me get through future difficulties and, above all, she believed me. If, just like Aladdin, someone was ever kind enough to grant me three wishes, one of those would definitely be that this doctor was still my doctor to this day and that I could make a carbon copy so that everyone had a doctor just like her! She was someone who was professional and very caring, someone who spoke to me and treated me like an equal, and someone who recognised that on the rare occasions when I went to the surgery it was because it was something important and she took the time to listen.

At the time though, my mindset was that I was stuck in this relationship without having the support network to leave. The support network was there however, it only needs to consist of one or two people to help you through. I just didn't see it clearly at that point, and didn't feel strong enough to take that plunge.

104

One time I did pluck up the courage to consider telling someone. I had bruises all up my arms which were caused after being struck repeatedly with an object. I was at work feeling lost and I'd got to the stage where I didn't feel I could cope with my life anymore, I just wanted it all to end by whatever means or form that took.

I didn't like the way that I felt, so I knew that I needed to speak to someone, but for me it needed to be someone that I trusted and had great respect for, and someone whose opinion I valued, because for me to open up and lay myself bare and vulnerable, I needed to be sure that it would be managed well and that it felt a safe enough environment for me to disclose what was happening. After all, if the disclosure wasn't handled sensitively, then my relationship would be the talk or gossip of the station and to have everyone's eyes on me, so to speak, would be too much for me to deal with; as a very private person, I would have hated for my personal stuff to become public. It was also a message that had been reinforced from my first day as a police officer: keeping your private life separate from your professional life was really important. I was conscious of the fact that I needed to distinguish between the two.

There was only one person that I felt I could disclose this information to, a person I trusted and had the upmost respect for. I was conscious of the fact though, that they were senior to me and very professional. They were someone that I looked up to for doing the right thing, but that filled me with dread also, as the right thing was that they might feel that they had a duty of care also, and that duty of care might have been to encourage me to make a formal complaint and get Jamie arrested. Was I ready for that? From then on the chain of events would've been outside of my control to a certain extent. It is often this fear of 'the snowball effect' which ensues after a complaint is made to the police, that prevents many victims from coming forward and getting the necessary help and support. After all, they, like me, just want the behaviour to stop.

The person that I trusted was on duty that day. I mustered up the courage at several points to walk towards their office, but each time it seemed that someone had just beaten me to it, or that they were on the phone, or that I would meet another colleague in the corridor and I managed to somehow get engaged into conversation, therefore the momentum and my confidence seemed to dwindle.

It got to much later in the day and I overheard the fact that they needed to go to a meeting at another station; I thought this might be my opportunity to speak to them away from the station. I decided to approach them and say that I needed to go over to that same station also, to speak to a particular officer involved in a case that I was actually reviewing, and would it be possible to

106

share a lift. That was my plan anyway, I didn't need to speak to the officer in person about the case, but it wasn't about that, it was about the opportunity to disclose to someone I trusted what was happening within my relationship, on the journey to the other station.

I timidly went into their office and explained that I needed to go over to the other station also, asking if I could possibly have a lift. Due to the fact that they were senior in rank to me, it must have seemed a rather odd request for me to have made. I got a rather puzzled look back; they said yes it was fine, but that they were not going for another hour. I said that was fine, of course I would have said that because it was the need to speak with them that was important to me. If truth be known, I would have waited several hours for that journey on that day.

I left their office feeling quite strong, though unsure of what might happen. Unsure of how or what I would say; I just knew the car journey might provide an opening for a conversation outside of police work, or about general chit chat, and then I would somehow blurt it out. It might not make any sense whatsoever at first, but at least I thought my nerves and anxiety would be overcome and I could at least get it out. I wasn't even thinking about the consequences or 'snowball effect', I just knew that if I was ever going to have an opportunity where I had mustered up enough courage to say something, it was on that day with that person. For me it could only be that person. In the meantime, I tried to focus on my work but couldn't. I felt so sick inside and my mouth was dry. Should I, shouldn't I, will they believe me? They had no reason to doubt me; I was a professional, dedicated officer, who always seemed to deliver what was required. I was hard working and motivated and was good at my job, and on top of that I was polite, courteous and no one had ever had a bad word to say about me. Yet doubts, such as a victim not being believed, are never far from your mind.

Would they understand what I had been going through, would I be able to describe or relay what was happening for them to know how much I was hurting and dying inside? Or would I minimise it, which is how I would often rationalise the behaviour in my mind, and in my everyday life, in order to cope. This time though, it was different because I had reached a point where I wasn't coping anymore. I knew it was only a matter of time before I would break. I kept looking at the clock, not that I needed to, because apart from the sound of my heart beating so fast, I could hear each second ticking away on the clock.

After what seemed like an eternity, the hour was up. Should I go to them, should I wait for them to come to me? While I was debating this, they appeared at the door with their coat and briefcase in hand, and yet rather than ask me if I was ready, they said that there was a change of plan as it actually made more sense for them to go on their own. They would be half way home and by the time they were expected to finish their meeting, it would be their knocking off time, so they hoped that I didn't mind. They would see me when they were next on duty, which was four days later. I said in 'typical me' fashion that it was fine and wished them a great few days off.

Inside I felt crushed; it wasn't their fault, they would have had no idea whatsoever what was going on for me, no idea what that journey would have meant for me. It was an opportunity, and that opportunity had just vanished in front of me.

Life for me has always presented learning curves, some positive and some negative, but out of this came the fact that, from that day forward, when someone needed to talk to me, or they went out of their way to engineer an opportunity, I always made time for them. Regardless of how much time, because they might just be at breaking point too, and if that opportunity was lost their next action might just be their last.

When I went home that evening, I resigned myself to the fact that perhaps there was no other way out for me. When Jamie went to bed, I sat downstairs for hours and I began to drown out the thoughts in my head with a bottle of Vodka. Not content with drowning out these memories, I wanted to block them out forever. I reached for the packet of Paracetamol and after a while I felt myself drifting away.

Chapter Six

Aftermath: Dealing with Reality

Did my need for privacy and professionalism impede my freedom?

My eyes began to open and I was unsure of my surroundings at first, but as I came around a little bit more, it registered that I was still in my living room. I was lying on the floor with the vodka bottle next to me and the packet of Paracetamol nearby. Looking at the opened packet, I had only taken about ten tablets. It was hardly going to make a difference in the scale of things; I couldn't even get that right at that point in my life. I felt pretty low at that point, coupled with the fact that my body had to deal with the amount of vodka that I had drunk, I felt so sick. The room seemed as if it was swaying, but the swaying was me as I tried to move. I thought to myself what the hell have I done? Has it really come to this?

I felt resigned to the fact that I was stuck in this relationship, with someone who was not only abusive and violent, but above all someone who was a bully. The majority of the overt things, I could generally work around or deal with in my mind, but it was the subtle things that seemed to penetrate more. The violent outbursts and acts of aggression were literally that.

In my case, I had experienced being assaulted many times as a police officer where I received pain and injuries. Some of these injuries ranged from bruises and cuts, through to substantial bite marks, debilitating back injuries, significant shoulder and knee injuries that have resulted in long term pain and disability despite operations.

Therefore most physical injuries I learnt to switch off from. Yes they hurt, some had a lasting physical effect and some will be forever with me as scars, becoming more prominent each year when the sun decides to shine, or I'm somewhere hot on holiday. However these injuries didn't penetrate me emotionally.

For some victims, however, their physical injuries do cause them emotional and psychological trauma and some physical injuries can dramatically change a victim's life and impact on them significantly and some scars are permanently prominent and on display, unable or difficult to be hidden.

For people who are suffering from domestic violence and abuse, each person's experiences, triggers and traumas may be different and unique to them. There may be similarities, but there will also be differences, as we don't all act, react and respond in the same way. This is based on our own individual learning, encounters, experiences and messages we receive.

It was the mind games that potentially could, and did, do the damage for me. The constant questioning of my ability to do things and of the words or opinions that came out of my mouth (until these words and opinions stopped and I began to withdraw, as I didn't see the point of engaging anymore). This may seem crazy, because I had a responsible job where I had to make key decisions, assess situations and act on them every day.

Being a police officer, as I'm sure is the case in other jobs too, is a physically and psychologically demanding role. It was like I was living two very different lives: the one at home where I was made to feel incompetent, worthless, unloved and a shadow of myself; and my other life was someone who was respected, treated as an equal and valued for my ability, my knowledge, experiences and above all my professionalism, and yet there were many times when the two separate lives seemed to cross over.

I can remember many a time having to stay late at work, particularly if a rape incident was reported to the station, because I was trained as a sexual offences officer. I would regularly be allocated to deal with the rape victim and this entailed taking them to a rape sympathy suite, being there to help the doctor

113

obtain medical evidence, gathering the evidence and sealing it up and then obtaining a lengthy statement detailing the events of the rape and any other information relating to this. This whole procedure could take hours upon hours, if not days, and it is painstaking information that is obtained and the whole experience of the police being involved makes it extremely traumatic for the victim to recount what has occurred. The account is often chaotic, so it is vital to take the time in order to piece it all together so it is as accurate as possible.

As a police officer, when you are obtaining a statement, you are trying to describe and paint a picture for someone who is reading that statement who wasn't there at the incident, as they need to be aware of all the information as if they could imagine being there. The statement therefore has to be extremely detailed. Obtaining such statements can, and often is, quite harrowing for the officer taking it, because you are absorbing all the information, in a traumatic and harrowing way. The last thing you want when you are taking a break, making the victim a drink, is when you have to phone your partner and inform them you are going to be late home, because of what you are dealing with, is to be faced with a barrage of verbal abuse on the other end of the phone, because you are going to be late. Then having to compose yourself and go back to the victim and carry on working with them, when inside you are trying to hold back your own tears, and wondering what will face you when you eventually get home.

This was such a regular occurrence for me that I would dread picking up the phone, my stomach would be doing somersaults and I would feel physically sick whilst building up the courage to call.

What kept me in the relationship was the fact that I felt emotionally and financially drained, and stuck in many ways! Like most other victims, I didn't think that I would be able to cope with leaving (as strange as that might sound) or manage on my own. Of course I had managed several times over when other relationships had ended, but the key difference was that my confidence and self-esteem hadn't been eroded to this extent or severity, as it had in this relationship. Confidence was so important to me and plays a vital role.

Living almost two very separate identities and lives was extremely draining. It seemed as if I was on a high state of alert at all times. I knew that I had got to the point in life where this high state of alert could only now be sustained for a limited period of time and at some point it would come to an end. At that moment though, I was just trying to cope, but just coping was beginning to take its toll on my immune system and my overall wellbeing. I didn't want to lose the little of myself that I had left.

I began to look back at my hopes and dreams as a child. What was it that I wanted to do in life?

First I wanted to make a difference. I still wanted to do that, but my relationship was holding me back and destroying the me that cared, not just about others but about myself too.

Secondly I wanted to be a police officer. I was already doing that so I technically had achieved that, but had I? I was turning up and, although doing a good job, I knew I could do more, deliver more and make an even bigger difference.

Thirdly I wanted to be able to be me and for others to respect me and perhaps love me for just being me.

I knew if I remained in the relationship I wouldn't be living the life that I wanted to live. I was sick of being kicked, and punched. I was done with being Jamie's emotional and physical crutch and battering ram. I was already dying inside and knew that if I stayed then this could at any point become an actual reality.

My parents had already lost two children just after birth and had a couple of miscarriages. They had always been so desperate for children. Therefore, I thought in that moment: what right did I have for them to lose another? It was at that point things

116

changed, thinking about those siblings that had died. I have spent many years since trying to locate their graves, not only for my parents who were told the records of the graves were lost in 1967, but also for myself, to say thank you to them for keeping me strong. At the end of 2012, I found those graves and I have visited and said thank you. I have since taken my parents to visit too, who have the opportunity this year to erect a memorial stone. Once again I will pay my respects and say thank you.

I came close to losing my life when Jamie's hands were around my throat. I had attempted to put an end to it myself on two occasions: once by trying to wrap one end of a telephone extension cable around a rafter in the loft with the other end around my neck, standing on the chair at the top of the stairs, but I just couldn't jump off or kick the chair over. The second time was with the tablets. Now though, it was as if something had switched on, not only in my mind but in my heart. I was determined that no one would have power and control over my life apart from me.

I got up the next morning feeling that I had nothing to lose. I was already at rock bottom. I packed a bag with my sentimental belongings and important documents such as my passport, driving documents and a folder with personal correspondence containing bank details and bill payments etc., and I looked back into the house and thought: it's time to take this opportunity. As

I hooked the lead onto my little dog's collar, I knew I had to make a choice. As I closed the front door, I had only one thought on my mind, "Life, do your worst because I'm ready".

Of course, I wasn't exactly ready, because I had no idea what was in store for me. I was holding onto the thought process that nothing could be as bad as being in that relationship, so anything else that I came up against, I would deal with and come through the other side. Great thought process, but realistically I had nowhere to go apart from into work. My little dog stayed asleep in my car in the police station car park. I periodically went out to check on her to ensure she was okay and I just set about doing my work for that day. It was as if I was trying to push it to the back of my mind, trying to blot it out, but I would have to face that fact at the end of my working day. Would another opportunity be missed; would I go back to the house before Jamie had got home and noticed anything out of the ordinary?

Looking back, I hope that I would have continued through with my decision. As fate would have it though, despite several colleagues coming into my office throughout the day, it only took one person to mention my bag and for them to jokingly say, "it looks like you're leaving home", and when my reply came back in a serious way that I was, they quickly changed into practical mode.

There started a chain of events, from being vulnerable in a violent and abusive relationship to being vulnerable as my private life was exposed for all and sundry to see, have an opinion on and to feel the need to offer a piece of advice.

The majority of people were generally well meaning, but there were one or two that were not and wanted information as ammunition to step over me, or attempt to at some later point in the future. There were questions circulating as to why should they, from now on, listen to me or take my advice as a specialist in domestic violence, when I couldn't even deal with my own stuff and that I was hypocritical. In a warped sort of a way, I thought at the time perhaps they had a point. Yet I was good at my job; I always tried to look at a situation from a balanced perspective, assess it and look at the options. I would never tell someone what to do, it was their decision. Obviously safety was paramount and I would point concerns or issues out, but whatever decision was made, I looked to what structures and strategies needed to be in place to assist them. Therefore surely my personal life should be separate to my professional life.

I was offered a bed at a colleague's house and I was offered the usage of sofas; all of a sudden I had a whole host of people coming out of the woodwork offering me a roof over my head. This was a great help for the short term, but long term I needed to think about what I was going to do because it wasn't just me we were talking about, it was my little dog too. People were lovely to me, but it's a difficult thing not feeling settled, not wanting to outstay your welcome, trying to make yourself seem invisible, but unable to.

I did recognise that being a police officer or working within the police 'family' was a privileged position to be in, for many reasons, and despite the bad press the organisation or people within it get, there are times when it closes ranks and pulls together.

At this particular point in my life, I did feel privileged because senior officers at my station felt that my situation warranted my name being put forward to be placed in police accommodation. I'd been in police accommodation on a temporary basis for a few months once before, but never thought they would be able to help me again. A number of police forces had a few police houses, or accommodation blocks which were called section houses, for officers' use if they were in financial or any welfare difficulty, for either temporary or permanent use. Such houses have been phased out by many forces now, but they were a lifeline to many in difficulty. They were also used when officers had to transfer to other locations within their force's geographical areas and hadn't sorted out selling their house or their future accommodation. In order for my name to be put forward, it needed the backing of senior officers from my station,

120

which they did. Lots of people don't have this help or support and I know how pivotal this intervention was for me, and for that I will always be extremely grateful.

Having access to accommodation is a life saver, especially for victims of domestic violence and abuse. Without access to this, many victims are forced to stay in the violent relationship, or are placed in or offered temporary accommodation. Some victims are able to cope with being in accommodation such as refuges or hostel spaces, but for some victims they return home as they are not able to cope with the difficulties and issues this presents.

It is widely recognised that if a victim builds up the courage to leave, but returns to the abuser, the violence and abuse escalates, as does the frequency of such incidents and the victim is less likely to keep reaching out for help from others, whether professional or personal. The importance of accommodation will always stay with me and played a key factor in me building up a property portfolio and being able to accommodate some victims of domestic violence in their time of need.

Although the accommodation was key for me, it also brought with it some financial difficulties. As a police officer, part of my salary included an allocation of monies for housing. This was in place so that, as an officer, you would not be on the streets in financial difficulty and therefore in a position to collaborate with the criminal element of society, which we had clear access to in order to make ends meet or manage. On one hand therefore, moving into police accommodation was vital, but it also meant that I would lose £365 each month from my salary and would therefore struggle to make ends meet.

The accommodation I was allocated hadn't been lived in for many years. There were no carpets, furniture, electrical items such as washing machine, cooker, or fridge. The windows were rotten in places, letting the cold air in. In some of the rooms there were hundreds of dead flies on the floors. Above all though, it would be a place of sanctuary and safety. I knew it would be a difficult journey, but this accommodation would give me the space for me to work out who I was and I could start to rebuild me. I was armed with my sleeping bag and my little dog and I knew I would be okay.

After a week or so, a work colleague approached me and said they had seen me near to where they lived and asked me if I had moved into one of the police houses. I told them where I was living and they said they would pop around at some point.

When they came around a day or so later, they realised that I didn't have any furniture, or even a bed. I felt embarrassed. They came back later that evening with a blow up camping mattress for me. A sound bit of advice came that night: I was told to let people in; to let those that wanted to help, help me, and that sometimes it was okay to wear your heart on your sleeve, because others will view you as being human too, and I would be respected even more for that. Being private was a big thing for me and I did hate everyone knowing my business, but I was asked whether in the scale of things it really mattered what other people thought, as those that like you will always like you for being you, those that don't like you will continue to dislike you? Of course the answer is that, in the scale of things, it didn't matter.

In the following months, I found some new friends at work and some existing friendships became much stronger. It was amazing to see how many people cared and genuinely wanted to help. Work colleagues, whether police officers or members of the support staff, really helped me through this period of my life, without them it would have been so tough.

My family and close friends outside of work were also such a strong support to me. Their bank balances must have been greatly dented by the cost of their phone bills. They offered unwavering support, often feeling at a loss to know what to do with the blubbering wreck on the other end of the phone. I wasn't sure at the time whether all the emotional turmoil was due to the realisation of the type of relationship that I had been in, whether it was due to the arrival of yet another bill, or statement highlighting being overdrawn, and wondering how financially I was going to manage; or whether it was from the fact that I felt lonely with my thoughts, when the working hour had finished.

When I was in the relationship, this kind of space was something that I craved. I wanted to be free from the behaviour of my partner and I wanted the noise and chaos in my head to stop, or at least subside. When I left and was on my own, I had finally got my space, but why wouldn't the demons go away?

I knew that I needed to distract myself with something. This technique had worked intermittently in the past, so I had to believe I could make it work this time. I needed to focus on what I loved to do and what I felt was important to me; so I needed to focus on being a great police officer and on making a difference.

Chapter Seven

Coping Strategies: Working for and against you.

Did my coping strategies work for or against me and were they always the healthiest of choices?

I needed to find a way to cope with the feelings that had bottled up inside me for many years. I wasn't prepared for the emotions or the feelings that were rising to the surface.

I wasn't one to openly wear my heart on my sleeve, but my heart felt so exposed and vulnerable and my way was to use alcohol to numb the pain and to silence the questions inside my head. I've heard way too many times over the years, people, including police colleagues, saying or insinuating that once a victim leaves a violent and abusive relationship then things will be okay for that person. That is so far off the mark on so many levels.

For some victims of domestic violence, the violence doesn't stop when they leave, because the perpetrator does not want to be left. The perpetrator sets out to find the victim, if they don't know already where the victim has gone. They attempt to track them down; they try to rope friends and family into this course of action, often by pleading their perceived case that they think they are the injured or wronged party, or that they are sorry for what they have done. They say they want to find the victim to make it up to them, or they offer up what they think are reasons, but are excuses, for their behaviour such as: the influence of drink, drugs, or the fact that they have no money, things are getting on top of them, there is a buildup of stress, they are struggling to cope, the children are playing up or being difficult and this put pressure on the relationship, that they were abused as a child in their own lives or the victim flirts with other people and that makes them jealous.

To the perpetrator these are all perceived reasons why they might be violent and abusive. They are in the habit of laying blame or attaching blame on any other person or thing, instead of looking inwards at themselves. We all can and often do experience some difficulties or issues in our lives, but it doesn't mean that we, each and every one of us, gets violent and abusive and takes this out on our partners. If I have a drink, I don't get violent or abusive; I just want to fall asleep! Other individuals under the influence get silly and just want to laugh and have fun.

All of these things are aggravating factors and may play a part, but they are certainly not responsible for the behaviour of the perpetrator. They are just excuses for the perpetrator to use, as if to divert the blame away from them. Sometimes the perpetrators

126

are so convincing that other people get sucked in or drawn into the perpetrator's rationale. They might even feel sorry for the perpetrator, so they share the information of the whereabouts of the victim and any children.

The perpetrator might beg for forgiveness and say to the victim that they are sorry. The victim might feel so confused, lonely and isolated with their own emotions, feelings and thoughts that they decide to go back to the perpetrator.

The majority of perpetrators that I have met over the years can be extremely charming, convincing and above all manipulative. Yes, we all have the capability and capacity to be charming, convincing and manipulative in our own rights, but a perpetrator of domestic violence has, and often does, take this to the next level, to boost their own power and control over another.

It may be that the victim does not want to go back to the perpetrator and the perpetrator might try the charm and 'sorry, I'll change' tactics first. If these attempts are unsuccessful then the perpetrator will often switch to being threatening and abusive and a victim can return very quickly into that emotional and psychological trauma.

Some victims will go back because they fear the ongoing harassment from their partner. They fear the vulnerability of not knowing when and if their partner will suddenly appear and threaten them, or cause them harm, so they will go back because a rationale is that at home they will be able to often see the violence and abuse warning signs, they may even be able on some occasions to diffuse the escalation of violence and abuse.

In some cases, once an incident of violence and abuse is over, it may be a while before the next outburst occurs, so the victim learns to deal with that outburst in the way that they specifically have learnt to cope, for example by shutting down their emotions to blot out what is happening or has happened in order to get through it.

For the victims that stay away, they will have to rely on coping mechanisms; even if the victims have no contact with the perpetrator, they will still need to rely on their coping mechanisms to deal with what has happened and the losses that they have suffered.

When you are living in a violent and abusive relationship, you use whatever techniques you have learnt, to block out the experience and memories so you can continue to function. When you leave and stay away from that relationship, there are often two ways victims react. They may continue to block it out and not deal with the emotions and feelings. For some, this might work, as they are able to distract themselves with something to

128

focus on, sometimes this focus might be the children, work or for some the cause of domestic violence. This can only be a temporary fix though, as it's almost like putting a plaster onto a cut; the type of plaster and the environment and other elements it's exposed to will determine how long it will stay on for, and whether it gives adequate protection for the cut itself.

The same thing happens by blocking out the emotions and not dealing with them. If you don't work through these emotions in a healthy way, these untreated and unresolved emotions will only resurface at another time in the future when you are faced with another painful experience, trauma and loss and the second situation will compound the first. Therefore even more trauma and emotions will be apparent.

The other way victims react is to use coping strategies to help them through the pain and trauma. Coping strategies can either be healthy ones, or equally unhealthy ones. Even if one particular coping strategy was healthy or worked for you at some point in your life, it doesn't mean that same strategy will always work and remain healthy.

One healthy way of coping might be to have a support network around, perhaps consisting of friends, family or colleagues and it might help simply by being around them, or by talking to them about what has happened or about how you think or feel. For some, being around those closest to you might not help as much, so it's about the trade-off; will these people be a positive or negative impact? If it is negative, then perhaps an alternative is to look to professionals to provide that supportive and empowering arena.

A support network doesn't even need to consist of loads of people, a starting point of one person would be good, but I wouldn't suggest that it is healthy long term to have just one person as your support, because sometimes they might have stuff going on themselves, or difficulties in their own lives and they therefore might not be emotionally or physically available for you. Therefore, it generally is deemed healthier to have at least a couple of people in your support network.

A constant support for me was my dog. I have always had a dog in my life; they are such loyal and loving companions. They want for nothing really apart from food, water, play time and your love and companionship. They don't judge you, or criticise you, unless of course you go away for a few days, or away on holiday, and in their eyes you have abandoned them as they see it. Then of course, you might get them sulking for a day or so, but after that they are back to normal. I don't think they ever stop loving you unconditionally, unlike their human counterparts. I have had a number of little dogs; sadly, with such shorter life spans than us, it is inevitable that a day will come when they will not be around. These loyal companions, though, have a dear place in my heart and remain in my thoughts and memories.

In difficult times, these companions have been the ones that have kept me sane and have helped me through, with a look of love and affection. When I have been upset, it's as if they have sensed it and they just snuggle into you, or brush up against your leg, as if to say I'm here for you, don't forget. I didn't forget and it would often be that little nudge or look of affection that would warm my heart enough to carry on. There were many a time when I felt so low, that I would get a hug from my little dog and in that moment everything would seem okay. One particular dog that I had, I loved with all my heart, kept me going and I would say that she was my rock.

Another healthy coping strategy is to seek professional help, such as Counselling or psychotherapy, to explore with you what has happened, to work with your emotions, thoughts and feelings, and for you to work towards healing and recovery. As previously mentioned, one source of support for me was my doctor, who believed me and took the time to listen.

Other healthy ways are to take control of your life and yourself, by looking towards a structure to work from. Most victims, including myself, describe the feelings of chaos, of needing to juggle everything in order for the perpetrator not to kick off, and yet this way of dealing with the chaos shows the excellent skills that many victims have of managing things to keep things calm. Some begin to work through getting back their own identity that they lost in the relationship itself, others may need help and support to work through this, from family, friends, colleagues or professionals.

For me, yes I made the decision to leave in the end, but it didn't mean that I was able to cope with it in a healthy way. I felt scared and lonely and I didn't feel that I knew my true identity any more. I felt lost and vulnerable.

I didn't seem able to move through that pain; I would get home from work and feel lost. If I had any spare money on payday, I would buy a couple of bottles of wine and I looked to blot out the pain initially with alcohol. I would have one or two glasses of wine and then go to bed. The wine seemed to blot out the pain not only in my mind, but in my heart temporarily, and I would sleep. The only purpose the wine served was to blot out the time at night, it would enable me to sleep and when I woke up it was morning and time for work, where I could distract myself with the work. Blocking it out at night wasn't helping me to deal with anything, because the difficulties were still there the next day, it just gave me some temporary respite; I knew I couldn't continue with that method and, besides which, I couldn't afford to.

132

One senior police colleague said to me after a few months that a way to get over a trauma or painful experience was for me to throw myself completely into work and that would give me a focus and purpose. I loved my work and I loved being a police officer, so I figured that their words of wisdom might be helpful for me. I began to do it; I was there at seven in the morning, then after my shift, would go home to see to my little dog for a while and then go back for a few hours.

I had a certain level of autonomy in my role, which enabled me to be flexible. There was always lots of work that could be done and my bosses would allow me to be creative with exploring projects and initiatives that would help address domestic violence. I didn't ever get paid for any extra time that I did, it was my choice to be there more than my standard hours. I was allowed to bank time to take off at some later point, but again I very rarely took it off, because I didn't want time off from work. At the weekends, I would go into work for a bit, so I could keep on top of my workload and then I would go back to the police house. There was an enclosed garden at the house, so I would do some gardening. Gardening for me has always been therapeutic; it's always provided me with the opportunity for the mental space for calmness. It's when I can chill out and switch off, in effect.

My parents had given me an old lawnmower and some tools, so I would cut the grass at every opportunity and do some weeding (sad, I know). I would also buy the cheapest and most colourful packets of flower seeds and try to grow them, to brighten up the borders to make it feel like a home. I would then sit in the garden, with my little rock, and try to work out what I wanted to do with my life and what direction I wanted it to go in. I wanted to find me again, the one that was funny and full of laughter, the practical joker in the family; I wanted to get back to being the healthier me.

Throughout my childhood, I was always sporty and fit. I was more often verging on the underweight category, not through under eating, but because of the amount of energy I would burn up. During the application process to join the police, I had to be weighed, because there was a minimum weight you had to be, as well as a maximum. Although hard to believe now, I only weighed seven stone, twelve pounds at the time; indeed I was verging on the underweight category, so I put on my heaviest clothes just to get through the weight issue.

Over the years, I've come to the realisation that when I'm in a relationship, whether a good one or a bad one, I have used and still use food as a way of coping with the emotional buoyancy any relationship brings with it and the emotions it stirs up. When I am single, there is no one close enough intimately to make me feel vulnerable, and therefore I don't turn to food to meet that need. For most of us, this association with food as an emotional crutch goes back to the messages from childhood, around if a child is hurt or upset an adult will buy that child an ice cream and, of course, it generally stops the tears in some way. Sweets and chocolate often have that same effect.

When I have been single in my life, I get back into the habit of being active sports wise and seem to take more care of myself and my health in general, and as a result I lose a lot of weight. In a negative kind of way though, my brain now associates losing weight with the pain and feelings of isolation initially caused from a break up, due to the weight which is lost in the first few months, as opposed to associating the weight loss with the gain in confidence it gives me and the true feeling of being myself and the ability to drive forward with anything I want to do in life - the 'world is my oyster' thought process re-invoked.

When I'm in a relationship, the weight goes on in a defensive way to protect me from supposedly being hurt. That probably makes no sense at all to anyone else, but for me this is how it seems. Whenever I am determined to lose weight, I do really well, and then it's as if I get to a point where I sabotage my efforts.

When I'm feeling low or vulnerable though, it has been a pattern for me to use food as a comfort blanket or emotional crutch and alcohol as both a way of coping with the difficulties and pain in order to numb things, and as a defence mechanism to block out any negative or vulnerable emotions. The two mechanisms or strategies certainly aren't the healthiest of options.

When I feel content within myself in general, within a relationship, within my work or life in general, I don't seem to choose either option as a way of coping or as a defensive mechanism. Instead, I utilise other ways of coping, such as gardening, exercise and sport. Crazy how our minds and bodies work, don't you think?

In the world we live in, we all have a level of access to information about what is healthy and good for us and what is not. Despite this information, and the knowledge that these unhealthy options are going to do us harm, we continue to still do these harmful things.

A similar thing happens with regards to being in a violent and abusive relationship: we know as a victim that staying in the relationship is ultimately doing us harm, but we stay for whatever reason or rationale that is going on for us as an individual, and we will all have similarities in our reasoning and rationale, but equally there will be differences too.

136

There are the difficulties of many other things that a victim will face upon leaving the relationship, such as financially how are they going to manage? What if there are children involved too, there will be the issue of family court involvement and the issues relating to access. Some victims of domestic violence don't want their children to see the perpetrator and are frightened and scared with having any form of contact, or permanent link to the perpetrator. Some perpetrators attempt to charm, convince and manipulate the people and systems within whatever agency, saying that the victim is incapable of bringing up the children, often raising the question of any unhealthy coping mechanisms the victim has used in the past. Funnily enough though, the perpetrator negates to also inform these agencies that the need for a victim to invoke such coping strategies or defence mechanisms might have been as a direct result of the perpetrator's behaviour. Funny that!

Whilst some victims of domestic violence recognise that the behaviour directed towards them is inappropriate, they can often feel themselves, or are made to feel, substantial guilt around the issue of letting their children see the perpetrator, especially when the said children are asking after the perpetrator. As children, some of them may not have the capacity to comprehend that the perpetrator's behaviour towards the other parent was unacceptable, although for most children they will be aware of the behaviour either directly or indirectly. The question for me

137

would be whether they see this behaviour as the 'norm' and think it's acceptable within the context. Therefore, the victim might be faced with continual requests by the children to see the perpetrator. As a result, the victim often feels as if they are perceived by the children to be the 'bad' parent. It is this guilt that can sometimes draw the victim back into the violent and abusive relationship.

For some victims who do not have a place to stay through family, they may seek the services of a refuge. Although there are many refuges within each country for women, the majority, if not all, of these are at full capacity and are running a service almost hand to mouth, with the lack of permanent funding and without the luxury of extra resources. For male victims within each county, there are a small number of refuges, but these are very limited in number and are sporadic in geographical location, so there is a need for them to seek the services of single-male hostels within their area.

Unfortunately, there still appears to be lots of debate in society as a whole, and also within a number of organisations, around the subject of male victims. There has been the opinion amongst some members of society, and from professionals, that male victims are often perpetrators attempting to even things out with a female victim, or there is the opinion that in the case of female perpetrators when the victim is male, that the female perpetrator is only acting out of self-defence.

A victim of domestic violence should be treated as a victim of domestic violence, regardless of what gender they are. Yes, there are going to be differences of experiences, but there will be many similarities involved regarding the nature of domestic violence, that is the same for all of us regardless of gender or any other perceived difference or experience.

What does continually upset me is the fact that these male victims are someone's son, brother or father. Do we really want a male relative or friend to be suffering in this way and yet advocate that domestic violence against them is not as important as it is when the victim is female - seriously?

If you are a victim of domestic violence, a genuine victim of domestic violence, would you seriously want someone else to be suffering, when you know how bad it can be yourself?

Equally for professionals working in the field, if you have seen the horrendous damage that domestic violence perpetrators can inflict on their victims, whether physically, emotionally, psychologically or sexually, are you seriously going to ignore the same plight of the male victim, or do you have a magic wand that will lessen its impact? I think not.

The sad thing is, society and the governments of most countries around the world are still not reacting quickly enough to the plight of male victims, which is the same way they both dealt with female victims: it has taken over forty years to even get to the place where we are now for female victims, which is still not good enough or acceptable; we still have such a long way to go.

Let's hope it doesn't take as long to get to the same place for other minority groups, who still seem to be some way behind, in the societal and government priority pecking order!

What message are we as a society sending out to male victims of domestic violence, when increasingly governments are pursuing policies, action plans and targets predominantly focused on violence against women and children; for me, it begs the question: what about male victims of domestic violence? In my twenty years' experience of dealing with domestic violence victims and perpetrators, I have dealt with a high number of male victims too.

When I first became a police officer, the number of males coming forward to report incidents of domestic violence against them was virtually non-existent. It was difficult then (and still is) to actually encourage female victims of domestic violence to come forward, given their significant concerns and fears. There are still many females today that still are reluctant to come forward. Awareness and support has improved greatly, but we still all have a long way to go with victims as a whole. For men, it was clearly happening also, but there was a great reluctance to admit it was happening to them. This was a mixture of feeling ashamed and embarrassed that it was happening, a vulnerability within their perception of their masculine identity, and a real fear of not being believed or taken seriously by professionals, family, friends and colleagues.

One male victim, standing in front of me with a cut to his head, covered in bruises, several bite marks, cigarette burns and numerous scratches and gouges caused by finger nails, who had sustained years of violence and abuse on many levels, was reluctant to make a complaint. He felt no one would believe him, as he was bigger in build than his female partner. He had never experienced violence or abuse previously in any other relationship, and he had remained within the relationship because ultimately he loved his partner and he thought things would change. Within his relationship, he experienced not only physical elements of domestic violence, but emotional and psychological abuse too.

Over the last ten years, the number of male victims of domestic violence coming forward to report incidents of domestic violence has increased. The latest statistics in the United Kingdom highlight one in six men are victims of domestic violence at some point in their lives. The statistics will still not reflect the true picture of those affected, as it will be an issue that is still under reported, as with female victims of domestic violence.

I have always advocated help and support for ALL those affected by domestic violence and a concern that I hold is that domestic violence is minimised within certain quarters of society enough as it is, without government and other key agencies adapting policies, funding and resources to fit under the banner of violence against women and children. It should be violence against women, men and children – as domestic violence as a whole should not be tolerated.

There is the need for services and resources to be broken down even further, regarding what support is out there for those in what society perceives or identifies as minority groups. How many refuges are out there for domestic violence victims who are from a black, minority ethnic community, or from the lesbian, gay, bisexual or transgendered community; then break it down even further, such as what about victims having a disability?

Certainly in the United Kingdom, as the definition has been amended to include sixteen and seventeen year olds, do we need specific refuges for that age bracket or can their needs be met in the same way as it is for thirty year olds, or sixty plus year olds?

142

There is the need for further awareness and education for professionals working in this field also to look at the wider picture. I have been told by a number of agencies over the years, including Women's Aid personnel, that they do not see a need for a separate service for lesbian women for example, as they are still female victims - really is it that simple?

What happens in group work when all the other female victims are talking about male perpetrators, how comfortable would a female victim, who had a female partner as the perpetrator, be in discussing her experiences?

Just because individuals are victims of domestic violence, it does not mean that they are not homophobic, racist, or have other prejudices, or indeed are not involved in any other criminal activity.

Just as some elements of society view male victims, there is a view that female perpetrators are not as powerful as male perpetrators, therefore the physical damage cannot be as serious. Of course it is serious, any physical abuse or violence is unacceptable. What some seem to do though, in the 'domestic violence professional arena', is associate different levels of impact or seriousness, dependent on gender or imbalances between a couple.

A bit stereotypical I think, and if we were all working from a stereotypical stance, then wouldn't emotional and psychological abuse and violence perhaps be worse coming from a female perpetrator where the male is victim or in a same sex relationship between two women.

I am sure there are millions of women out there who have experienced controlling and coercive behaviour from their male partners. Yes, there needs to be a generic overview for those involved with dealing with domestic violence and abuse in order for them to have a starting point and some guidance, but each individual case will still have its own uniqueness, based on the victim's experience, messages around relationships, values and beliefs; and not all perpetrators are the same either, they have their own differences and similarities also.

Unless some of these concerns are addressed, then these mixed or unequal messages, discrepancies or gaps will continue to prevent some victims coming forward and getting the appropriate help from organisations and other elements of society that they so desperately need.

Some victims may go to organisations, but feel discriminated against, or feel that their experience isn't being taking seriously enough, and overall, feel they are not being believed. Then that would be enough of a message for some of those victims to return to their relationship with the perpetrator, where what they see is what they get, with a view of 'it's perhaps better the devil you know, than the devil you don't.'

In turn, if a victim doesn't get the appropriate help and support or doesn't feel that they have received this, it only reinforces the message that most perpetrators use to keep the victim at home, under their control and prevent the victim from reporting it to agencies or organisations, which is the message that the agency or organisation, or more to the point the individual worker, won't believe them, won't help them and won't take it seriously.

Bingo perpetrator wins! And the victim is more reluctant to, if ever, leave the perpetrator and seek help again in the future.

If the appropriate messages are sent out to the effect that help is out there for ALL victims and their individual needs will be met, then this will encourage more victims to come forward. However, the services and organisations will need to be true to their word and deliver such a service, because if a victim does build up enough courage to approach such a service or organisation to seek help and the resources or support are not actually adequate enough in helping to support them with their unique experiences, then the support network element, as part of their healthy coping strategy and mechanism, will not be there. A way of coping with this vulnerability will perhaps be for them to go back to the perpetrator and/or turn to unhealthy coping strategies and mechanisms, such as alcohol, drugs, crime or in some cases turn to suicide to block out the trauma.

There is substantial research out there in the academic ether, to confirm the links between domestic violence victims and alcohol abuse, domestic violence victims and substance abuse and domestic violence victims who turn to crime, either because their partner has forced them into carrying out that crime, or that they are seeking to escape the domestic violence home life and see prison as a way out. There are a significantly high number of female prisoners who have a history of domestic violence being perpetrated against them; also there are significant links between domestic violence victims and mental health issues ranging from anxiety, post-traumatic stress disorder, self-harm through to suicide as a way out.

If the appropriate support services and resources are not there for a victim, including support specifically tailored for their unique experiences, then the consequences, not only on the victim themselves but on society as a whole, are extremely high.

I thought about leaving my relationship many times, but it took years to come into fruition. I thought of all the possible ways I might leave, but never felt it could become a reality. I spent years hoping that a miracle would happen and that perhaps

Jamie's behaviour would change, but it never did it just escalated and got more frequent and severe.

The longer I stayed in the relationship, the more it took away from me. Piece by piece, I was losing me, losing my strength, my confidence, and it was not only affecting my physical health through the injuries received, but also my emotional and psychological health.

To leave, I had to take the opportunity that presented itself when I felt strong enough or determined enough in a way, but strangely when I felt at my lowest ebb. There had been other opportunities where I could have perhaps left, but didn't, because at those points I felt low but I wasn't strong enough to leave.

So I knew on that one day that I had to pack my bag and leave. I had no idea whatsoever how life would pan out for me, but at that point I wasn't sure I cared. I just couldn't cope with being in the relationship a day longer.

Leaving and stepping into the unknown was outside of my comfort zone. Not only the fact that I felt so alone inside and so low, I felt lost, not only in the environment and in the world itself, but within my identity. It was the taking away of me that I found the hardest to come to terms with. It has taken a long time to find out who the real, true me is, and each day I still keep on learning more about myself and my capabilities.

If it wasn't for the support of my family, my work colleagues, friends and my little rock in particular, the immediate six months and the following two years perhaps would have turned out much different.

It is so important for a victim to receive the help and support that is right for them, not only in the immediacy after a victim leaves, but for the time it takes for them to begin to rebuild their strength and for them to have the space to think about what has gone on and what they want to do.

You cannot always make such key decisions that will change your life in the spur of the moment, or after an incident has happened, because there is too much chaos, not only around you in your environment, but also within the mind.

In the first few weeks after leaving, that's why the bombardment of texts, messages, visits and approaches by the perpetrator, either threatening or saying they are sorry, is so intense: because often the perpetrator is frightened that if you as a victim are given the space and opportunity to be away from them, they fear you will not go back.

The threats and risk factor goes up significantly when a victim leaves a domestic violence relationship, that's why the appropriate support and help is vital at this time, not only from a safety and practical perspective, but also whilst the victim has the space to be supported. So the space works for them as opposed to against them, i.e. the space might make a victim feel lonelier, isolated from the perpetrator and missing them so much they will go back. And yes, if they make that decision it is their choice, so for the space to work for victims it is important and vital for the agencies and organisations, as well as family and friends, to support them and any children.

For me, initially the space made me feel lonely. I knew in both my heart and mind that it was the right decision for me and that I had to stay strong enough to follow through with it. You need to be strong to deal with what leaving any relationship brings emotionally, psychologically and practically, regardless of whether violence or abuse has been present, and the fact that leaving a relationship also brings with it the practical and financial implications. In addition, when it is a domestic violence relationship, there is the fear element, having an eroded level of confidence and self-esteem and having been fed the messages that you will not be able to cope on your own.

Financial and practical matters play a significant role for most, including me. I had financial commitments like everybody else; I had to pay for my accommodation and for all the associated bills that came with it. I had a car to get me to and from work, again cars bring with them ongoing overheads. I had credit cards to pay; these had built up and I would continue to pay them off, but equally I would continue to use them, as when I was low I would buy little things to cheer myself up, trying to buy myself happiness to cover up or deal with the pain. Of course it doesn't work and it's no excuse to spend money that you don't readily have, because all it does is just add to the problems or difficulties in the long run. I didn't live a lavish lifestyle by any means.

When I left, the financial arrangements didn't go away. I still had the to pay for the accommodation which I had left, because I was tied into a lease agreement, and in addition to that I had lost the subsidised accommodation payments from the police due to being placed in a police house. I now had the responsibility of paying for two lots of accommodation and two lots of bills, until it was all sorted. If accommodation, whether rented or yours through a mortgage, is in your name, or in joint names, you have to pay the bills until they can be changed, stopped or any outstanding amount is cleared. If you stop paying them, it doesn't matter what the circumstances are, you end up getting a bad credit rating and it will affect you in the future.

I couldn't stop the bills from coming through my letter box, even the council tax bills for both properties. I tried to stop the utility bills that were in my name, but the bills that were in both of our names I couldn't stop or take my name off them without Jamie's agreement to do so, and of course they wouldn't do that for a long time. Therefore, until a partner agrees, you are both technically responsible for those said bills.

As a result of all of this, as soon as pay day came, which was once a month, I barely had enough left for the essentials. I guess I was still lucky as some don't even have enough for the essentials. For me, my shopping consisted of things that I could make last all month: a packet of toilet rolls, a box of Weetabix, a bottle of apple and blackcurrant cordial juice, a Tesco 'value' big packet of pasta and a tube of pesto sauce.

Some months, when I had skipped my cereals at the beginning of the day, or skipped the pasta at the end of the day, the previous month's food would last even longer, therefore I didn't need to buy more, and on those occasions I would treat myself. This would consist of visiting the local butcher who did an amazing deal at the time: I could buy a large tray of chicken for ten pounds. So, on a few paydays, I could get one of those and I would add that to the pasta.

In order for me to be able to buy my monthly shop, I would walk everywhere I could, even if this meant a one or two hour walk. For any of you who have to do this all of the time, I apologise if it seems lame, but for me initially, it felt as if I had taken a massive step backwards in my life, my independence was something I had worked hard for, so not being able to use my car in the way I had, felt like a failure to me - of course in the scale of things it is not, but at the time I struggled with it. Even now, if anything happens to my car, I get anxious as it shakes my independence. It was a tough time, though I'm sure that I had more than some people to eat, and I knew deep down it would be okay and worth being in that situation to be free of my partner.

I knew also that I was in a more fortunate position than victims who have children, because I didn't have that tie or connection. I didn't therefore personally experience the tug of war that goes on with the children, the one where some perpetrators use the children for the sole purpose of keeping in touch with the victim. Some sadly have no interest in their own children and when they do get time with them they don't do anything, or they may cast them off to another relative or friend; or they do the complete opposite and spoil the children with gifts, so that they enjoy spending time with the perpetrator, and then the children share the fact that they get spoilt with the victim who then is made to feel guilty for not being able to spend the same on the children.

Of course, in the long run, what is healthier for the children is the fact that they are safe from witnessing and/or experiencing the violence and abuse. Some children don't always see this at

152

the time though. It also depends in the children's eyes as to how the parent who is the victim is managing, or not managing, to cope. The children are also often used as pawns to pass messages from the perpetrator to the victim, and more often than not the messages are extremely negative, and these might question the victim's ability as a parent.

It is vital that there is a support network available for the children also, and this support network might consist of entirely different people to the ones that might be in the victim's support network. Sometimes children want someone who is not directly linked to the parent to talk to, and they want someone who will not feed information back to the parent, so it might involve a child's friend, or their friend's parents, a teacher, or a support worker.

Sometimes, it might seem when there are agencies involved with the separation, specifically when they are looking at the welfare of any children, as if they are working against the victim rather than for them. What these agencies have to bear in mind is the overall welfare of the children and generally these professionals should have experience and knowledge of what domestic violence is, what it entails, and the complexities it presents for all involved, directly or indirectly.

There are also outreach support services available for victims of domestic violence, and this work also involves projects and work specifically focused on any children.

It is vital that children get the help and intervention too; otherwise the impact and effects that they have witnessed and or experienced, if left, will resurface at a later date and will have hindered or prevented them from growing and developing to their best potential.

It is a myth to say that all children who witness and/or experience domestic violence through their childhood or adolescent years, go on to become either victims or perpetrators because, as I have said previously, we are all different, but there are a significant number that do become victims or perpetrators, to stress the impact and effect that it might have.

Children are not stupid, they don't just see and hear things, they can also sense when there is an atmosphere too. They watch out for the warning signs. They look out for signals of behaviour, tone of voice, actions, and they also look to the adults, their parents or Carer s, as role models and from whom they establish how they themselves might handle and deal with emotions. That's how we as children learn to find our way in the world: initially we watch our parents or our caregivers, then our extended family, then we watch our teachers and our peers at school and then as adolescents we look to our social network, and finally we might begin an intimate relationship.

If the environment where we initially learn how to handle and deal with our emotions isn't a safe or healthy environment, then unless intervention is made in that child's life, at the time or at some late date, it may and often does have a damaging effect.

One way of helping children to cope with the impact and effects of domestic violence, is to look towards professional help such as Counselling services specifically aimed at children or teens, or to approach other organisations involved in domestic violence to establish what projects or initiatives they might be running that might help your children. If these organisations don't run anything themselves, they should certainly be able to tell you who in your geographical area does and carries out key intervention work aimed specifically for children.

If you think of the emotions and feelings that a victim might have, or have had, as a result of their relationship, then think how difficult it has been, or still is, in trying to negotiate their way around why their partner was violent or abusive; think about the shame, the guilt, the trauma and turmoil they might have felt, blaming themselves, thinking "if only I'd have done something different." Look at how it has or did affect their confidence and their self-esteem, look at how it has changed their interaction with others, were they wary or withdrawn - then think of the children, the majority of these things they will be feeling too, and often the person they would most want to speak to about it, or to confide in is the victim, but because they see and feel their parent's pain and despair, they often don't talk to them about it, because they don't want to burden them with what they perceive as their stuff, so instead, if there is no support network for them, they turn that pain, trauma, experience and memories inwards and this can be a factor as to whether some of them find themselves later down the line as a victim or perpetrator themselves.

If, however, a victim doesn't feel that the professional help and support from any agency or organisation is appropriate and is having a negative effect, then it is also important for them to speak to someone about it. If they think something isn't right then to try to challenge it. If a victim hasn't got the strength to do this themselves, perhaps they could look to someone to help them with this dilemma. Support Workers, or Independent Domestic Violence Workers, are there to help victims through the process, and may, with the victim's consent, be able to go with them to some of these other organisations or agencies or on their behalf.

Another port of call might be to link in with the police domestic violence unit and ask for their help and support. Police Domestic

156

Violence Liaison Officers (DVLOs) are the link to many other agencies and if they cannot help a victim themselves, they will no doubt be able to put the victim in touch with someone who can help them.

For information on the type of agencies that might be able to help, why not look at my website: **www.tinaroyles.com**

Another useful contact to have when, as a victim, you feel that you are faced with an uphill battle, perhaps with the family court process, social services, the police or the criminal justice system, is your local Councillor or Member of Parliament (MP). They are there to help their constituents and represent them when there is a difficulty or challenge. There have been lots of occasions where I, in a professional capacity, have approached a Member of Parliament, to get their help and support with one of their constituents and, more often than not, the Member of Parliament has come up trumps. I am not saying that all Members of Parliament will be the same, but if you don't ask, in my opinion you will never get. It has to be worth a try, right?

It is vital and paramount that any victim, along with any children, get the support and help for them to find healthy ways of coping. In order to cope, I kept on in the knowledge that surely one day it would be better, and that the only way from rock bottom would be upwards.

Chapter Eight

Picking up the pieces: Negotiating my way through Domestic Violence.

Domestic violence for me is like when you drop a vase on the floor and it shatters into lots of different pieces. Some pieces, you can easily find and glue back together. Other pieces, you put back together but they are so damaged that the vase will never be the same again. Some pieces are lost forever. I equate these pieces of the vase to my heart, my identity, my personality and the very essence of my being.

Leaving my relationship was like a second chance in life, one that I did not want to squander.

I began to focus on what I had wanted to do with my life. Yes, the most important thing to me was being a police officer and focusing on improving the work around domestic violence, helping to make the services and provisions better for victims and children and to put things in place to help all involved. That was one of the main things I did to get myself back on track; what I thought would help me to recover from my own domestic violence relationship - focus on my work.

Some people within a therapeutic environment would call this focus a type of 'distraction' technique and say by doing this I wasn't addressing the emotional and psychological abuse that I suffered. Yes, I am aware of that now, but at the time I wasn't. I just wanted to get on with my life and for the painful memories and trauma to subside and evaporate.

In truth, I knew I wasn't then ready to go there and explore; I know I wasn't strong enough within myself at that time, to deal with the can of worms that exploring it would have opened up for me. So I focused on my work and I also focused on me, for the first time in a very long time. I decided that I wanted to get back to the healthy me and the one that had fun.

I knew that I wasn't going to get healthy by doing nothing, as life is never that simple. My mum was getting a new push bike and wanted to get rid of her old one. Riding a bike wasn't my idea of fun. It might have been okay when I was a child, but the police years had taken their toll and I had sustained a few injuries after being assaulted dealing with incidents (domestic violence police incidents, incidentally); I had been left with a badly damaged kneecap and the ligaments and muscle were affected also. It was like a 'catch twenty two' really, because I needed to exercise for the ligaments and muscles to strengthen, but in turn this would cause more pain and additional damage to the kneecap.

I decided to take the plunge and get the bike from my mum. At first, every weekend I took out the bike for an hour first thing in the morning. I took my little dog with me in the beginning, holding onto her lead whilst she would run alongside the bike, but there were too many times where I came off trying to avoid her crossing in front of me. She was a little dog that just always wanted to be right by my side, regardless of what I was doing; such a beautiful and loyal little dog.

Instead of stopping the exercise though, which would have been easy for me to do, I decided to carry on with it on my own, and then, when I got back home, I would take my dog out for a walk and sometimes, if I was feeling energetic, we would jog a bit also. It got to be that after a few months I had built myself up from wobbling along on the bike, to doing a five mile ride at the weekend, followed by a one or two hour walk. If the weather was okay, we would perhaps spend the day walking. I loved those times we spent together out in the fresh air as if we didn't have a care in the world.

Of course the bills were still coming through the door, but I had equally taken the plunge and decided to face those demons too. I arranged to have a meeting with a personal advisor at the bank. That was a scary thing for me to do because I hated dealing with anything relating to finances, but I'd realised that when I had more structure to my life and the things that I did, at least I knew where I was and was perhaps more in control of it. I was not able to bring in more money, but what the personal advisor helped me to do was to set up another bank account, which was specifically for paying my bills out of. I had my current account where my wages would go into and then we set up a standing order to go out every month to my new account, which we named my 'bills account'.

I changed all the bills that I had to direct debits and all of these came out of the 'bills account'. We had worked out what all these bills came to each month, so that the fixed amount that was transferred each month would cover all of these.

Although the money I had left in my current account was only a small amount, I knew what I had to play with for food, toiletries, petrol and anything perhaps unexpected.

It was like a weight off my mind, structuring the finances, and I felt like I was more in control of it. I also found that some weeks, if I was careful, I could go to the police bar and begin to socialise a little and build new friendships.

When you get into a relationship, friendships are often the things to suffer at first, as a result of you wanting to spend time with your new partner. Most of us do this; it's kind of natural at first to want to spend every possible waking hour with the one you love. When your role is the friend, most of us kind of take this hibernation on the chin as a minor inconvenience, because we expect it to subside at some point in the not too distant future, and for the relationship to regulate and the couple begin to re-establish their old friendships again, or to build some new joint ones.

With a relationship where there is violence and abuse present, your old friendships seem to be part of the collateral damage. Generally, because these friendships are yours and, more often than not, your friends love you for just being you, they are protective over you.

In essence, those friends are a threat to your partner. Your partner will therefore either begin to play up when they are around, such as sulking and not engaging with them fully, acting as if they (your partner) are better than your friends. Your friends might get pretty miffed at this and might confront you and say that your partner isn't the right one for you. At which point, you might take your partner's side and begin to step away from your friends or your friends will begin to withdraw themselves away from you and your partner.

On the other hand, your partner might begin to pull out all the stops and lay on the charm offensive, being over familiar and over friendly with your friends, so much so that they seem more like your partner's friends than yours, and you just tag along. This isn't because your partner wants new friends; this is because your partner wants to manipulate and begin to control your friends, meaning in the long term for you to become more isolated from them.

At some point in the future, your partner might tell you that one of your friends gave your partner the 'come on' and again you will start isolating yourself from this friend perhaps, and your partner will look like the hero/heroine, when they say they won't be friends with these people anymore out of loyalty to you.

A different tactic might be to play up so much before you go out to see your friends, by sulking or making you feel guilty, that you stop going out because it's easier to keep the peace with your partner. Whichever way it happens, you begin to lose your friends, who have been your support network; and the one who loses out the most, is you.

There is only one winner and that is your partner.

An abusive and violent partner might also use these techniques with your family because, like your friends, these are people who are generally on your side (although some families are not) and they will be a threat to your partner, because potentially your family, like your closest friends, might be able to help maintain your strength, to see through your partner's behaviour, manipulation and control and then you might leave. Whereas, if your partner is able to isolate you from your family, just like your friends, then you will be more dependent on your partner and in turn you will be more vulnerable, to be manipulated and controlled to better effect.

Again, another way is for the perpetrator to pull off the charm effect, and win over and integrate themselves into your family and build up such a rapport with them that your family see them as a wonderful partner, and aren't you the lucky one to have such a person in your life.

For me, I had friends through work, but ended up not socialising with them whilst in the relationship, because every time there was an event where Jamie would come with me, my partner made it quite clear to everyone that they didn't want to be there. They would make rude or insulting comments, trying to sound funny and slightly sarcastic, so not completely overt. It made people stop and have to think about whether they had just been insulted or not, therefore making it extremely awkward.

At some nights out, Jamie would say that they'd had enough and ask for the car keys to sit in the car. I would be on edge not knowing if they were in fact sitting in the car, winding themselves up because I hadn't left straight away as well, or whether they had driven off and left me at the event so that I would have to find my own way home. Of course, it could be either of these options, and it happened enough times to warrant me to stop accepting invites to events out, or having to make excuses for not turning up at the last minute.

At first, I challenged the behaviour and tried to stand strong, but eventually it tires you out so much, the not knowing, the walking on eggshells, the scenes and the awkwardness of it all, that you begin to withdraw from everything.

The friends that stayed with us throughout the duration of our relationship were therefore either Jamie's friends originally, or they were joint friends that we met together who were predominantly Jamie's friends first and foremost.

Did they see Jamie's behaviour? Of course they did, but they just seemed to brush off the fact that sometimes Jamie could be obnoxious, arrogant or rude, because on the flip side, Jamie could be the life and soul of the party. When Jamie was in that holding court, funny and charming frame of mind, everyone wanted to be their friend. It was as if the friends were tolerating a naughty child, who had been laughing and playing one minute, and then throwing teddy out of the pram and playing up the next. These friends just seemed to take it in their stride as if it was the 'norm' and for me it began to become the same.

Everyone else seemed to accept it, so why didn't I? That's how it was. It just wasn't that simple because, although I was living with this behaviour and on the surface accepting it, underneath it had an impact on me.

I was nervous and on edge most of the time, never knowing when a scene or outburst would occur and never knowing when I would be left red faced through embarrassment. Never too sure when I would be left stranded, never knowing when I would be left picking up the shattered pieces.

When I left, at first I had no immediate contact with our joint friends because I didn't want Jamie to find out where I was. They knew where I was working, because it's not that easy to move your work, but I couldn't guarantee that the joint friends wouldn't show their complete allegiance to Jamie, and let them know where I was.

At work, I felt safe because it was a police station and if I was going to feel safe it was going to be there, so I didn't want to change my working location. It didn't help that I had to walk to places due to petrol money being short, but I would try to walk off the beaten track, not on the main routes, or where I thought Jamie would drive. I would walk through some of the estates, or on the cycle tracks; not the safest course of action for anyone, so I wouldn't advocate anyone else to do that, because these are the

166

places where in particular women are targeted for sexual crimes or muggings, and it's not just restricted to women - anyone could be a target for crime at these locations in this day and age. For me though, the focal point was avoiding Jamie at all costs, as I didn't want to bump into them, I wasn't focused necessarily on other safety issues that could arise and I was perhaps putting myself at risk from a vulnerability perspective during this time.

After a few months, I bumped into a few joint friends. I didn't give them my address but arranged to meet up with them occasionally, until it got to the point where they would bring up Jamie's name so often in the conversations that it was clear they were either being asked to drip feed information or they were on a fact finding mission. I didn't want to play any part in that; it seemed more sensible for me to distance myself from them, as opposed to leave myself exposed and vulnerable. So that's what I did - I let go of all the joint friends and began to focus on my work life and me.

What I realised from my partner's behaviour, was that they were just like a bully. They could, during our years together, manipulate and control me. They were comfortable with being violent and abusive towards me, but they were not brave enough to take on my work environment now. They appeared to try at first, because there was an occasion when one of my bosses came in to see me. He told me that Jamie had been into the station and it wasn't the first time they had come in trying to get to speak to me. Due to the jungle telegraph being in place at most work venues, most knew there had been issues, therefore Jamie had been referred to this boss and he had dealt with it for me. I asked this boss what had happened and he said that it was nothing for me to worry about, but that if I was approached I should let him know.

What he did say to me during our chat on that day though, was something that I have held quite prominently in my memory: that I wasn't to become bitter, and that not everyone was like my ex-partner, and for me to not to shut myself off from the possibility that in the future, someone would come along who was a really decent person and would treat me the way I should be treated. He was a lovely man, and like many colleagues or bosses during my service and since, has risen quite high up the ranks of the police force.

I was very lucky to have some amazing colleagues and bosses. You get to see some real qualities of human nature when you work within a police force. You see courage, real resilience and true compassion and passion. There is this 'family' experience or bonding. It's often hard to describe to other people who are not in such organisations like the police, the army or the fire service or other emergency type services where you have to really rely on each other in the most difficult and unsafe situations, but if you are in a position where you come out of such an organisation, you really notice not having that 'family' support around you, and it is a massive loss in its own right.

Just as society reflects human nature, so does the police force; potentially there might equally be some rotten apples within the police, not only in the role of police officer, but in the role of police staff also. Unfortunately it is often these rotten apples that can give the police such a bad name.

If you cross such rotten apples in a working environment, as well as other environments, they can and do make your life a misery. I came across a number of these rotten apples in my working life. Some have been dealt with, some have not.

For these rotten apples to be removed or dealt with, first of all it relies on someone with a sense of smell that will detect the turn of the apple, and then it will rely on someone opening the bag or barrel of apples and deciding to tackle the rotten one, as opposed to just taking a peek and shutting it off and hoping it will fix itself. Of course, if there is a rotten apple in a bag, the rotten apple doesn't turn into a good apple again on its own, it requires treatment. If it is left untreated, it goes on to potentially infect the other apples in the bag, slowly turning them one by one, and eventually even the healthiest of apples in the bag have the potential to turn rotten. If you are the one who tries to tackle the rotten apple on your own, you get exposed to the negativity, and you sometimes might get tarred with the same brush. You might get told to leave well alone, as it's not your place to tackle it, as other people get paid for that. People join the crowd and look away. Yet, left untreated the rotten apple can do significant damage and someone has to be brave enough to delve into the bag, or put their head above the parapet.

Several times in my police career, and outside of it since, I have been in that position where I have had to stand above the rest, and put my head over that parapet, especially as a grievance adviser. Let me tell you, that sure is a lonely and isolating place to be. If you do it, you risk everything apart from your core being. You have to weigh up the trade off, because ultimately once you put your head above the parapet, it has the potential to backfire, and if it backfires, it will certainly have an impact on your own health and wellbeing so much so that, as a result, you might have only one option left and that is to walk away.

For me, in any environment or capacity, those that bully or intimidate have some of the basic traits of a domestic violence perpetrator. They use their words and actions, including silences, to manipulate, control and intimidate a victim or target. They too might be verbally abusive or harassing at first, and then it may move into the realms of physical or sexual abuse. Others around may be aware, but keep their heads down, not wishing to get

170

involved, thinking to themselves that thankfully it is not them on the receiving end, or not them anymore, who is the victim of bullying. They may smile at you in a knowing way, but they won't take action themselves. Some will collude with the bully, whether intentionally or not, often through their own insecurities.

When you raise the issue of bullying, often everyone goes silent; then, some will mutter their disapproval of the behaviour, some will tell you not to make a fuss because you will be the one to come off worse, some will say if it was them they would tackle it head on, but of course you know if push came to shove, and the shoe was on the other foot, they wouldn't dare tackle it.

When you do raise it, and get knocked back, because the support or resources in place to deal with such things are sadly lacking in what they promise, and you attempt to tackle it on your own, you really notice that you are on your own. If you have mustered up the strength to do it and stand above the parapet, there is no question that it will zap all your energy and it will be a rocky ride, but deep down you'll know in yourself whether it was ultimately the right thing for you to have done.

Whenever I have put my head above the parapet in my life, I have taken a long and hard look at whether it has been the right thing for me to have done. I have not rushed into the decision or made any rash moves, and I reflect on it afterwards as well. To get to a point where you raise something like that, or take action, it already has been a hugely impacting process, and you know you're in for some flack and turbulent times. Ultimately, if I had to make those decisions again, I would take the same action. It may take me some time to raise it, and the impact on my health and wellbeing might be significant, but it would have been worth it for my own sanity, firstly, having made the decision in the first place and, secondly, to follow through until the end, whatever that end might look like.

Keeping focused on my work, I began to build up the Domestic Violence Officer's role into one that was not only productive, but a vital cog in the wheel within the police force. It was important for the role to work, so that it would not only stay in place, but for it to expand and develop further. I have helped hundreds and hundreds of victims of domestic violence and their families, both within the police and on leaving the police, and there is no greater reward in life than to be in such a privileged position, where you can help empower someone to take action, which in turn may save their life and that of any children.

There have been far too many horrendous cases that I have dealt with within the police, and also upon dealing with the aftermath and long term effects and impact within my private practice, so that I know you cannot always protect yourself from soaking up the emotions that you see. There is a constant need to keep yourself, as a practitioner, safe and healthy emotionally, psychologically and physically, and as such the use of supervision is pivotal in ensuring practice is safe for victims and clients and well as yourself.

As a police officer, after a traumatic incident you are able to access the welfare department and have Counselling. Most police officers won't do this, as historically they have been wary, and still are wary, of this process, because it is an in-house mechanism for help. Whereas, when you are in the role of a Domestic Violence Officer (or other specialist areas where you deal with continual trauma), there were a number of sessions that you were allocated as part of your role each year, because of the recognised impact the work would have on officers carrying out such a role.

Again, as with other areas of specialism within the police such as Child Protection, Family Liaison and Sexual Offences, there is a risk of impact of the trauma experienced.

Additional roles to my permanent role of Domestic Violence Officer were as a Family Liaison Officer and a Sexual Offences Officer. I was able to manage my health and wellbeing within these roles by doing sport or spending hours in the gym, as a way of an outlet. This kept my mind clear and focused, but also made me feel confident because I was keeping myself fit and healthy as well.

I am a firm believer in doing things to the best of my ability, and I am in a stronger position to do that when I feel confident in that ability. There are two things in life that put me at an appropriate confidence level for me to be able to do my best, and they are, firstly, I am able to arm myself with information on the issue or subject and gain the appropriate knowledge and experience, and secondly, I do not let anyone chip away at my belief that I can achieve.

There are always people in life that will fail, or are even unwilling, to achieve their own hopes, dreams and aspirations, and rather than them keep getting up and trying again and again, they become a defeatist and wallow in self-pity and become bitter and envious towards others that may want to achieve. They will chip away with any negative comments, or make subtle jibes to make the other question their quest. This is often purely about them and their own insecurities. They might be jealous of your determination and passion, and when you begin to succeed they will try to muscle in on your success, as opposed to making their own way or success in life, and I have met plenty of them in my time also.

Before I met Jamie, my confidence had been up and down in life, up as a child through sports and laughter, down through some childhood bullying, up with my focus on joining the police, down through the difficulties in police training, and up again through my work.

An example of my confidence level being in tip-top shape, and when there is no one around me to chip away with negativity, is when I first joined the police, when within my first month of my chosen career, I was asked by my force to take part in the 'Service of Thanksgiving to Celebrate the 150th Anniversary of the Foundation of Essex Police'; this service was to be held at the Cathedral in Chelmsford and was by all accounts to be packed out, due to the fact that they'd sold hundreds and hundreds of tickets. Not knowing of the magnitude of the event, or indeed how significant this 'Service of Thanksgiving' would be, I said yes.

There would be five people reading from the order of service that day: the first readings, which were from the orders and instructions framed and issued for the government of the Essex County Constabulary in 1849, were read out by me, Constable Tina Royles, the person who followed me was the Chief Constable, and then a Police Sergeant, followed by Her Majesty's Lord Lieutenant for the County of Essex, and finally The Lord Bishop of Chelmsford.

There I was, all 7 stone 12 pounds of me, standing in front of all of those people, including my mum and dad; I was a very proud but nervous person that day, but my mum and dad were also very proud too, which mattered greatly.

Two days prior to the Service, whilst I attended a practice rehearsal, I was approached by one of the then Assistant Chief Constables, who asked me whether any of my family were attending the event to see me. I stated that they lived in North Wales and that I didn't know I could invite anyone. He said he would organise two extra tickets for them on the off chance, but that I was to at least telephone them and give them the opportunity to attend if they could, as it was to be a significant part I would play in Essex Police History.

When I left the Cathedral, I went straight to a telephone box in Chelmsford (it was before the days of mobile phones so I had to ring and wait for someone to answer and then feed what pennies I had into the machine). Fortunately my mum answered and I told her what the Assistant Chief Constable had said. It was a Friday night and my dad was still at work until 8.30pm, but she would speak to him, though she was doubtful that they would be able to attend at such short notice and it was a very long way for them to travel. They had only been to Essex once before and that was to drive down with me in my car the month before, to make sure I got to Essex safely to start my career. We only had time

176

for something to eat before they both caught the train back to north Wales. Anyway, she wished me good luck for the service and I said I would phone her on the Sunday night after it.

After my phone call to my mum, I can remember going into Habitat to look at some furniture for my accommodation. The weekend before, I had picked up the keys to a studio flat which I was renting from a colleague at my station, and all the studio flat had in it was a wardrobe and a single bed that my sergeant on my shift had given me. In Habitat, I saw a coffee table and a wooden chair, but was unsure whether to get them or not, so I decided I would sleep on it. The next day, I went back to Chelmsford Habitat and picked up the table and chair. I spent most of the afternoon looking around Chelmsford, just passing the time, and it was about five thirty, as the shops were closing, that I left Chelmsford and made my way back to where I was living and began to make a start on building the table and chair.

These flat pack things take time to put together (for me they do still) and it must have been about nine o'clock that night when there was a knock on my door; I opened it to find my mum and dad standing there. I was so excited to see them; I know it had only been about a month, but for me such a lot had happened in that one month and here they were in front of me, it was amazing that they were there. Dad had worked an early shift on the Saturday and had managed to swap a rest day around so had got the Sunday off, so they travelled down straight after his early shift and they would need to travel back after the service the following day.

After the hugs and catch up, it dawned on me that there was just a single bed in the studio flat so, bless them, after travelling all that way they had to both share a single bed for the night, and I had a sleeping bag on the floor, but it was worth it to have them there.

The next day, I was dressed in my best 'parade' uniform with my white gloves on for formal police events. Mum and dad were in their best 'Sunday suits' and off we went to the Cathedral. I wasn't able to sit with them, because I had to sit at the front with the other speakers.

I sat there in the front row, looking down at my paper with my reading on it. It had lots of commas all over it where I needed to stop and pause, in order to convey my words and meaning appropriately. It wasn't me who did this, but a chief officer at the rehearsals on the Friday said it was a good way for me to emphasise my words and they wanted me to come over as confident and audible. I've worked to that principle ever since, I put a comma where I verbally pause, and to emphasise my meaning. What I end up with in essence is a piece of writing looking much like this book, with commas all over the place. I knew I was first on to speak after the hymns, fortunately in one way for me, because then I could sit back down and breathe a sigh of relief and take it all in.

I remember the Lord Bishop of Chelmsford call out my name and I knew that was my cue to walk to the pulpit. The paper in my hand was shaking, but using both hands I lay it on the stand, I also put my hands on the stand to steady my nerves, and I took a deep breath and thought - just do it, what's the worst that can happen?! I have that ethos now when I'm public speaking or conducting any form of training. I'm always, without exception, as nervous as hell, but in the wider remit of things, I think - just do it, because it's worth it. The words came out as if it were someone else echoing them: my voice was powerful and strong, and the acoustics in the cathedral were amazing. I just focused on the back of the cathedral as far as my eye could see, and focused on an area above people's heads to speak to, then focusing again on my paper to get the next set of words.

When I'd finished, I collected my paper and walked down the steps back to my seat, and that's when the magnitude of the event hit me and the butterflies were in my stomach. It was another achievement in my life of which I am very proud.

When it was over, I caught up with my mum and dad. The Chief Constable and the Assistant Chief Constable came over to me to congratulate me on my professionalism, and after being introduced to my parents, they thanked them for coming such a long way to show their support and said they must be very proud of me. Of course my mum and dad said that they were, but I knew it was true because their little faces were beaming full of pride, which made me proud too. We then went off to a reception for the dignitaries, with champagne and canapés - both my mum and I had a glass of the old champers to soak up the atmosphere, and then we headed back to collect their things from my flat and they headed home. Thank you so much mum and dad for your love and support over the years, it never fades but just grows stronger as the years go by.

So, as you can see, when I'm feeling confident in myself and don't have anyone chipping away and eroding my confidence and self-esteem, I feel as if I can do anything. I don't think that I'm untouchable, but I believe in me and I feel that the world is my oyster once again.

Being involved in the service helped to keep my confidence and strength up for another few months; it needed to be, because police training at a National Centre is tough, very tough. You are put through your paces physically, emotionally and psychologically, to see if you can handle being a police officer and the difficulties and aggression that may be faced from the public.

My work on shift also helped to keep my confidence up, because with each new day and situation, I was learning constantly. It was exciting, daunting, very exhausting and, above all, such a steep learning curve, not only about myself but about life and people in general.

It is the little achievements and taking stock of those little everyday ones that, when you are in a difficult place, keep you going and moving forward. With me, it is also the big events and achievements that helped restore my confidence too, such as the 150 year service for Essex Police.

One of many significant achievements throughout my police domestic violence work was being the chair of the domestic violence partnership forum. It was set up by Chris Bainbridge, who set about pulling together strategic decision makers in key agencies and organisations from the voluntary and strategic sectors, such as Victim Support, Women's Aid, Local Authority Housing, Solicitors and Social Services. They all had an interest in ensuring that domestic violence would be focused on and that policies and procedures would be looked at, and that they would work from a monitoring and coordinating position. This was an important piece of work by Chris, because it was a long time prior to the government setting specific targets around domestic violence. What it gave us was an excellent platform to work from and to build up strong relationships with key partner agencies.

Chris Bainbridge also set up a domestic violence monitoring group within Harlow division, to ensure that all cases of domestic violence were monitored and were dealt with appropriately where possible. To enable this to happen, she established the voluntary roles of the 'Shift Expert' whereby an officer on each shift would monitor the domestic violence cases which that officer's own shift team attended and dealt with. It was the Shift Expert's role to give advice to colleagues on what action was to be taken or, if such appropriate action was not taken, to attempt to address this, and if this was not possible, to raise this with Chris Bainbridge and bring to the notice of the monitoring group.

Not everyone was on board with this initiative initially, but I for one thought it was an excellent way forward in raising awareness, and trying to get some sort of best practice spread out across the division. I was given the role of Shift Expert on my shift; no easy task I might add, but an important one.

When Chris left our division and moved on to another, she asked me to take over the role of Chair of the Harlow Domestic Violence Forum. It was an amazing opportunity for a police constable, because this position would have ordinarily been taken on by an Inspector or above, and the other agencies' representatives were at a level of Chief Executives and other management positions. For a while I felt daunted by this task, but it wasn't really about the responsibility, what counted in the end was my level of practical experience, my knowledge around domestic violence and ability to get us all working together off the same page. I knew, even at that time, that domestic violence couldn't be addressed or tackled to the maximum effect if each agency were to continue to work in isolation, working on different agendas, or pulling against each other. The way forward in my view was, and remains still, to coordinate the response - it's definitely what's needed. My ability to be creative and to think outside the box also helped with my credibility within the partnership group and therefore I was accepted as the Chair.

In whatever environment that I have worked in, I have always been told that I am balanced in my views and approach. It has been this aspect of my personality and professional attitude that helps me to look at the wider picture. It has always been important for me to look at the involvement of all within domestic violence. Why all involved have got to the point at which they are at. What are the dynamics that are playing out? What options are available for each of them, and what support and resources are available?

The first thing for me to do was to ensure that we, as a group, got the message out about domestic violence, not only to agencies, but to get the message out there to members of the public, firstly about what domestic violence was and how it could impact directly or indirectly, providing information on what agencies could do to help.

One of the things I consistently heard when I spoke to victims of domestic violence was that they had already been passed from pillar to post trying to find some support and advice. That worried me, because I already knew that it was difficult for victims to reach out in the first place, to build up the courage to phone someone, a complete stranger at the other end of the line, and to utter those words that they were being hit by their partner, and/or they were in a relationship where there were terrible arguments and they didn't know what to do or which way to turn.

How many of these victims might have put the phone down and thought no one wants to help me? How many of them might, after being put through to the wrong department or on being told it's not our organisation that can help you but try phoning so and so, then not find the continued strength to phone the next person, feeling as if no one cared. To me this was unacceptable.

184

We set about changing that, by sharing key information which had details around the range of key organisations that could help people regarding domestic violence, which not only had the key organisations' contact details, but also a screed of what service each organisation provided and what support they could offer.

The reasoning behind this was on reading the information, the victim might be able to ascertain which organisation they needed and telephone them direct, finding the appropriate support on the first telephone call as opposed to the seventh or eighth. This information was also extremely useful for professionals within the organisations, so they were aware of what other organisations could offer. It was also useful information for police officers to have and give out to victims of domestic violence; this information was also sent out to doctors' surgeries, hospitals, solicitors etc., so service users of those organisations could seek help.

Providing information on what services were available also became an integral part of the process of the Domestic Violence Repeat Victimisation and Offender Scheme, which I introduced within our police division. It was a scheme that was introduced to ensure all victims of any domestic violence incident that came to our division's attention, or which officers were called to attend, were entered into this repeat victimisation and offender scheme.

Level One was for a first incident, where both victim and offender received a letter confirming an incident had happened; within their letter, the victim received information around what domestic violence was and what agencies were out there to support them and giving the officers' details that attended and a reference number. The letter that was sent to the offender confirmed that the incident had occurred and it outlined what domestic violence was and reinforced the fact that police took it seriously and provided help information with regards to aggravating factors.

Level Two was for a second incident; again a separate letter was sent out to both victim and offender, which provided help information for both and stated that their respective area local beat officer would attend to see them both separately and provide advice and support, but also reinforced the stance police and other agencies took on domestic violence. The beat officer would also give the victim the information booklet with agencies/organisations' details.

For Level Three, the victim and offender again received separate letters stating that the Domestic Violence Officer would arrange a visit to see each party, to ascertain what further steps needed to be in place to address the behaviour and to provide help and support. Of course, it didn't always follow that the starting point

186

would be Level One; if the Domestic Violence Officer who saw all incident reports of domestic violence needed to invoke Level Two or Level Three immediately, then that would be done.

What did happen through this scheme is that all victims that came to the attention of the police within Harlow division received information on domestic violence. They also received help and support information, as did the offenders, and at Level Two and Level Three both victims and offenders had a visit from their area beat officer and subsequently the Domestic Violence Officer. Through these interventions, more awareness was raised, more intervention was taken and also there was an improved monitoring of the incidents themselves and an improved and coordinated way police dealt with the incidents.

It was always important for me to look for gaps in any of the services provided, and the role of a full time Domestic Violence Officer within Harlow division actually came about because of a piece of work that I did around the gaps in service and the way police dealt with domestic violence itself, whilst I was in the voluntary role of Shift Expert.

I was spending time recuperating from an injury in what was called the Crime Desk. It was an office dedicated to looking at all reported crimes, and the Crime Desk officers would see all the paperwork related to an incident of crime (when a crime is reported to police, a form which was called a crime complaint was completed, and this crime complaint as well as an incident report and any subsequent paperwork would be sent through to the Crime Desk), to ensure the incident and crime had been dealt with appropriately and that if someone was responsible for that crime, that all enquiries and investigations were completed and that, where appropriate, a person responsible was arrested.

Whilst in the Crime Desk, I began to see different ways that some officers would finalise a crime, not having exhausted all avenues of investigation, or matters might have been left outstanding, so I thought to myself - if this is happening for crime in general, what about incidents of domestic violence, what about the crime complaints that would come under this specific area? So I started to look into it, at first briefly, but then found it was a significant enough issue to warrant serious time to research it.

I knew that during my working hours this might not be possible to dedicate the appropriate time to it, so for a number of weekends I went into work on my rest days to do this research with the approval of my temporary supervisor. I wasn't claiming any time back, and I wasn't looking to be paid for that time. I just wanted to look into it and to help improve things and make a difference, if I could.

188

I know there are lots of people out there that want to make a difference but don't have the opportunity to be able to spare any of their own time to do this, but I know myself that if I want to do some of these things, then sometimes it might have to start with me giving some of my own time to it, to show the relevance and importance, and then perhaps follow up action might be taken. This is what I did. I did the research and listed all the crime complaints that I felt were outstanding but had actually been finalised, and I gave examples of what could be done in order for an offender to be dealt with and in turn enable the crime to be detected.

Detected is when a crime has been committed and the person responsible has been dealt with in a positive way, by whichever means available, whether they received a warning, a caution or were prosecuted through the criminal justice system. I knew that the senior officers within Harlow division, as within any division within any police force, are interested in crime and the detection rates: that's how they are rated on their performance and that's what they work towards.

I knew that if I could highlight a clear way to improve the detection rates for what came under violent crimes, then that would help provide more credibility for the issue of domestic violence. I submitted an in depth piece of work highlighting the issues and explaining the process of how, if monitored, the detection rate would improve.

A short time after submitting this report through to senior management, I received confirmation that because of the work that I had done, the command team at Harlow division decided that they would create a new role to help address these issues - that role was a full-time Domestic Violence Liaison Officer position (DVLO). Due to the fact I was on recuperative duties, I was given the opportunity to deputise for the Domestic Violence Officer and then when the role became vacant I applied, was successful and was able to take over the role permanently.

Here is an excerpt from the letter received from senior management regarding the domestic violence statistics and management information:

Dear Tina,

Thank you for the excellent domestic violence information and monitoring package which you prepared recently. You obviously put in a great deal of effort, much of it in your own time, to produce such informative and helpful material.

I am sure that the information you produced assisted in the decision-making process which led to the Command Team's decision to appoint a full time DVLO.

I have no doubt the system you have pioneered will be taken up by them.

Once again, thank you for the initiative you showed in 'seeing what was needed' Well done!

It was important to raise the awareness of domestic violence and another way to do this was by planning conferences and getting the message out to a wider audience. My motto was 'if you don't ask, you will never get'. I therefore began to ask celebrities to take part in these campaigns or conferences, in order to bring the issues to the media attention to enable the messages around domestic violence to get out far and wide.

At one conference, I was fortunate to be able to get Nadia Sawalha to attend, who was a very popular actress and also a television presenter and was therefore known to many at that conference. I was also able to approach, with a colleague, the local college and get the students from the graphic design and art course to design some posters around domestic violence and the three voted the best by the domestic violence forum would get work experience placements and also vouchers for their efforts.

Their posters would also be printed and used in a publicity campaign within Harlow division; in addition, the posters were sent out to all pubs, clubs, schools, businesses, doctors' surgeries and anywhere we thought would benefit from these posters, including public toilets.

For another conference, I was lucky enough to get the actress Simone Lahbib to attend. She has starred in many successful television series, including 'Bad Girls', 'Monarch of the Glen' and 'Wire in the Blood'; her attendance gained the interest of not only the media, but also raised the profile within the agencies that attended. It also heightened the awareness within Essex Police too, as I had invited one of the Assistant Chief Constables to attend also, as well as senior officers from within Harlow division.

Here is an excerpt from a letter received from the Assistant Chief Constable:

Dear Tina,

I thought the conference was a great success, which it deserved to be as it was well organised and covered all of the important issues.

Well done - an excellent day! I will be in touch.

What also came out of that conference was a request from Simone for me to create a 'help and guidance' information package for Simone's website, due to the nature of enquiries that she received from her fans. Again, it was another way to get the information out there to help and support victims of crime, particularly victims of domestic violence and other traumatic events.

Here is an excerpt from a letter received from the Assistant Chief Constable regarding the help and information package for Simone's website:

Dear Tina,

Thank you very much for sending me a copy of the web help page you have compiled. I am extremely impressed with what you have produced and have no doubt that it will be of assistance to those who access it.

Excellent work - well done!

As well as opening up the door to conduct training for many agencies, not only within Harlow division, but also on an Essex countywide basis, I saw a gap in awareness and training for the magistrates. I mentioned my concerns to a key figure in the Magistrates' Association at the time, and was able to share with them my thoughts on how to address this by delivering training to them. The magistrates had a number of key dates set aside each year when they all got together as a collective and I was to be allowed to take up one of those days to provide a training day on domestic violence.

Magistrates play such an important part in dealing with the cases brought before them, and to think that such an association, just like many other agencies, had no specific training around domestic violence was difficult to comprehend. Especially when about a quarter of all reported violent crime was of a domestic violence nature. To be given the opportunity to provide such training was a massive step forward.

Delivering this training brought with it a responsibility onto my shoulders for me to get it right as, if I had this one opportunity to speak to and provide training to the magistrates on the subject of domestic violence, the dynamics and complexities, then it needed to not only raise their awareness, but to also educate them to make more informed decisions. Above all, it needed to hard hitting and honest.

When victims and children are experiencing domestic violence, it is a terrifying experience and sometimes in the cold light of day, when the facts and evidence is being relayed in a court environment, the words written on the statements can and are

194

often devoid of emotion and the reality of the situation. The level of the violence and aggression, or any other acts, can and often are played down or minimised, because that's how most victims are able to 'box off' the experience, in order to process and deal with it. It doesn't mean that the impact isn't massive. Also, the perpetrator will minimise the level of behaviour or their actions, because they, more often than not, don't want to be punished for their crimes.

As a police officer, you gain specific insight into this terrible set of circumstances, the reality of it, and the magnitude and devastation you cannot escape, because often you attend in the process of this behaviour happening. You see and hear the shouting; you see and hear the violence; you see the terror on the faces of the victim and any children; and you see the aggression of the perpetrator, indeed quite often you, as the one there to intervene, get caught up in the violence and aggression.

The times when I have received life impacting injuries have ironically been at such domestic violence incidents, and the violence doesn't always solely come from the perpetrators, although predominantly it does. However, a victim sometimes believes that if a police officer gets involved and arrests their partner, in the long run this might bring additional difficulties for them, so sometimes a victim will turn on and assault the police officer out of pure panic, or out of a showing an allegiance to their partner, so therefore the hatred from the perpetrator is diverted onto the police officer, as opposed to the victim.

In practice, the injuries and attacks on police officers at the scenes of domestic violence incidents are significantly high, and such incidents provide a heightened element of risk attached to them. So some hard hitting video footage was called for that day at the magistrates' training; not to overtly shock them, but because there were some people out there in society that didn't want to know about domestic violence and who turned a blind eye to it (some still do), but in a professional role, professionals shouldn't turn away from the reality. They had to be aware of what it was like, in order to deal with it appropriately, as opposed to dealing with it in a blasé manner.

What I was trying to do with the video clips, and with my directness about domestic violence, was to get them to see or have some kind of empathy or realisation of what that incident might be like for a victim or any children.

I also put more of me into this event than normal, if that were possible to do, because it was important to get the message across of the devastation and not only the short term, but also the long term impact domestic violence can, and does, have on those directly or indirectly involved.

From that day onwards, the Essex Magistrates' Association has had a rolling training programme on domestic violence, not only for all new magistrates, but for magistrates on an ongoing basis. What I learnt from that experience is: never be afraid to ask if you want to make a difference and to improve something, sometimes you have to be hard hitting when necessary to really reach your audience, but then at other times you need to be sensitive and mindful of such an impact.

It goes back to the words of the necklace that I bought for my eighteenth birthday from my Nan, around accepting the things you cannot change, the courage to change the things you can, and the wisdom to know the difference.

I wasn't in the Domestic Violence Officer's role to win friends, I just wanted to make a difference and improve things. I did however recognise that by me being in that role, I could influence people around the issues relating to domestic violence within the police, within other organisations and for victims, children and perpetrators, and that's what kept me focused and driven to keep coming up with new ideas and initiatives, to try to address and combat it.

I was also lucky that my work around domestic violence was brought to the attention of the then Chief Constable, by the senior officers at Harlow divisional headquarters and by other senior representatives from other partnership organisations, on not only a local basis, but also on an Essex countywide basis, and as such, I subsequently received from the Chief Constable a letter of appreciation, which is an achievement in the 'police world'. It's not something as an officer, you think you will ever get, because in one way you are just doing your job. However when recognition is given not only in a verbal way, but in a written format from your senior officers, it makes you feel valued and appreciated. To get such recognition for your 'bread and butter' work from the main person - the Chief Constable, it felt amazing, not only for being valued and appreciated, but it was bringing the issue of domestic violence to the Chief Constable's attention.

Here is an excerpt from the letter of appreciation from the Chief Constable:

Dear Police Constable ROYLES,

It gives me much pleasure to write to you concerning your role as Domestic Violence Liaison Officer.

I understand that you have been instrumental in forming Domestic Violence monitoring groups at Brentwood, Epping and Harlow, organising publicity launches, raising the profile of Essex Police and have shown dedication to the post you hold.

This has led to a significant increase in reported incidents and seen the successful introduction of a repeat victim/offender strategy.

I have been made aware of the efforts you have made, in presentations to community groups, in your flexible working and in the number of letters of appreciation received.

Your professionalism in your role has brought credit not only to yourself, but also to Essex Police - well done.

Your Service Record will be endorsed accordingly

As a direct result of the Chief Constable being aware of the work that I was doing around domestic violence, I was able to go to important meetings and also participate in key training courses on his behalf, which again opened me up to a new level of knowledge and experience, of which I am very privileged to have had the opportunity presented to me.

The fact that some of the Assistant Chief Constables and other senior figures in Essex Police were aware of my work meant that I was able to suggest and push forward and implement key work to make a difference.

What I have learnt very much through my domestic violence work, especially within the police, is that it really does matter what you put into your work yourself; if you are professional, dedicated, motivated and passionate about it, you really can make a difference and change and improve things.

Yes, there are often obstacles on the way, including people who become jealous of your work, reputation and credibility, but if you really believe in yourself and the importance and relevance of what you are doing, then keep going, because you will achieve what you want to achieve and the majority of the obstacles can be overcome with creative thinking or a fresh approach.

The biggest obstacle generally that is in most people's way is themselves. For me that is definitely the case - my obstacle is my lack of confidence and in order for my confidence to go there is generally another person involved, chipping away at it.

Chapter Nine

Relationships: Testing the water and learning to trust again

"You can search throughout the entire universe, for someone who is more deserving of your love and affection than you are yourself, and that person is not to be found anywhere. You, yourself, as much as anybody in the entire universe, deserve your love and affection." Gautama Buddha.

The messages we get fed about relationships when we are children begin with fables or fairytale type stories. Yes, most of these tales have wicked witches or evil characters or creatures, but most end up with a fairytale ending as the prince or princess, the hero or heroine, or Mr or Mrs Right, turn up on a white shiny horse to save us. They sweep us off our feet, they lavish us with affection and love and we live happily ever after.

The reason most of us get disappointed in life with relationships is because we still live in the hope that one day our Mr or Mrs Right will appear, but this sadly is only reserved for fiction, or fables, and in real life, if we find love then we are lucky and that is something to be cherished.

If that one such person does enter into our lives, we need to go into a relationship with our eyes wide open to the fact that one person cannot meet all of our needs and expectations.

In order for us to be most content in life, we need to start first with ourselves and not only begin to love ourselves but to also like ourselves too. It took me a long time to get to the point of loving and liking myself. Yet how could I have expected others to love me previously, if I wasn't able to love myself? I thought that, if I could get confident with my own ability and like me for being me with all my strengths and weaknesses, then I would in turn become more content and, if I was content with myself, then I would begin to love myself too.

I started to look at some of the key values that I held, began to look at those which I felt were important to me and were important in my life. These included my views, opinions, principles, judgements and standards of behaviour that met with my expectations.

What did I expect from myself and what did I expect from others? The reality of life is that others may not have the same principles, the same values or beliefs. No one is a carbon copy of you, therefore chances are, if you are hoping for someone to live up to the same standards as you, then you are going to be disappointed every time.

In a working environment, what was important was that I was professional and gave of my best. Not everyone has the same outlook, some people turn up for work, do the bear minimum, to a mediocre standard and then leave at the end of their clocking out time, or some don't show the same level of respect or courtesy to their colleagues, the bosses, or members of the public. That can be difficult, if you yourself are professional and want to make a difference, because as a whole you don't have control over anyone else apart from yourself. The only person you can control is yourself, and your reactions to other people's behaviour or actions.

Once I recognised the fact that I had no control over someone else's behaviour and recognised the fact that another person only had control over their behaviour and their reactions to mine, my mindset shifted from worrying that I might have done something that triggered their behaviour, to thinking whatever I may or may not have said or done, your reaction is your matter and not mine.

It was like a huge weight had lifted off my shoulders. All I needed to focus on was that I lived up to my own expectations and that I alone lived up to, and stood by, my own values, beliefs, standards, morals and principles.

Of course, what I needed to do was to work out whether these expectations, values, beliefs, standards, morals and principles were mine, or whether they were my parents', society's as a whole or the police forces'. It was about reviewing where I stood on things, re-negotiating with myself about what I myself believed, getting rid of or discarding messages or things that weren't solely mine, and creating a new script for myself as opposed to the one perhaps given to me.

Once I had worked out what was mine to own, with regards to my beliefs, values etc. I felt a lot more at ease in the world. What was more important to me was that I was able to leave some baggage behind. I didn't need to hold on any longer to 'my story'; I could leave it behind and write a new one. This freed my mind to focus on the things that were important to me: my work, family, close friends, my dog, and of course myself.

Working out what was important from a values etc., perspective was so important because I had never really sat down and spent the time working this out before in any great detail, apart from when joining the police of course. I had never had the space, the knowledge or the need to before, but it gave me a clear picture that Jamie didn't meet these things at all.

When the time came for me to meet someone else, I now had a kind of template with which to work from. Easier said than done I know, because when your heart takes over, it can rule your head. However, at least I had some idea of what made up the core of me and it was at least a starting point for me to vet any potential partner.

It wasn't as callous as it perhaps sounds, I didn't pull out a sheet of paper with tick boxes on it, but in my mind that template was at the forefront.

One of the most important things for me was to be able to find someone who had good communication skills. Most people have the ability to talk, but what I was looking for was someone who would talk with me, not at me, and who wouldn't just talk about themselves; someone who cared enough about me, to ask how my day had been, or who wanted to know what my views or opinions were on things.

One of the difficult hurdles to get through or over for me, was to have the confidence to speak about myself with friends and to share my views and opinions, because Jamie had always reinforced the message that no one wanted to hear what I had to say, so I eventually ended up not actually saying anything and being withdrawn in myself; in effect that just gave others the impression that I did not want to engage with them, or that I was rude and unsociable.

I had a voice in the beginning of that relationship, but it got so worn down by the verbal abuse, criticisms and insults, that my self-esteem and confidence went too.

Even now, there are certain situations which I find myself in where I feel extremely uncomfortable, and my default mode still goes into withdrawing. Sometimes, I am able to stir myself out of this and make myself talk, or at least start up a conversation with someone, but this is after spending time building myself up to the conversation, and if the opportunity to intervene in a conversation doesn't arise or I miss my slot to speak, my build up process sometimes has to start right at the beginning again. I prefer it when there is a natural opening or break in conversation, as opposed to a 'put on the spot' one, because I need to have built myself up to it.

In a bizarre way, if I'm the one conducting training, then I know I'm going to be asked questions, but I will have prepared well enough to be able to answer, especially when it's training on domestic violence.

It's the same when I am asked to do a radio interview, if it's on domestic violence and/or relationship difficulties, the answers to the questions are often there on the tip of my tongue, I just have to take a pause and be clear on what I'm saying, and yes, even some radio presenters try to trip you up, but I try as best I can to stick to the point that I have made and repeat it.

So I can do that, but when I'm put on the spot in an environment I don't know, or on a subject I don't know, then I cannot seem to get my words out or my thoughts clear enough to make sense. Therefore, within a relationship, it's really important that a partner doesn't make me feel uncomfortable in any way, especially in conversation. Of course, there will always be times in any relationship where the couple do not see eye to eye, or have the same opinions, but it's important for both individuals to respect each other enough to be able to listen to the other and to take into account their views and opinions. It doesn't mean we have to agree all of the time, because we don't just morph into the other person when we get into a relationship with them. It is important that we hold onto ourselves within a relationship.

That doesn't mean that our views and opinions will remain static throughout life or during our relationships, but it is vital that we have a choice and are not forced into someone else's ways. It is also really important for me that the tone of the communication is appropriate, so for my partner to speak in a calm and assertive manner, which is clear and concise, but in a manner that isn't one which repeatedly gets louder and louder as a way of talking over me, as if drowning my voice out. I want to be able to engage with and feel comfortable with the one that I'm supposed to love.

A sense of humour is another important thing in a relationship for me. I have a very dry sense of humour and have historically in my life, apart from the years spent in my abusive relationship, been the practical joker, always seeing the funny side of things. So humour comes up very high in the list of things. Not humour at everyone else's expense, but one that helps you negotiate your way through the difficult times in life.

How many of us, when we are feeling low, might hear or see a comedian on the television or radio and we feel our mood lift up and our day brightens up, even if temporarily, or if you are in a serious kind of mood and something daft happens in front of you, you perhaps cannot help but crack a smile, or even erupt into laughter, the kind which makes your stomach ache with laughing so hard. So laughter is important for me.

An emotional connection is really important for me too. If I feel safe and secure, not only physically, but psychologically and emotionally, then I feel more comfortable with being myself. I guess that I'm no different from anyone else in that I want someone to love me for being me, not an idea of who or what they want me to be. If someone chose me initially for being me, then why would they want to change me?

Unfortunately, this is exactly what happens in the majority of relationships, where one person wants to change the other, or mould them into some kind of replica of themselves. For the majority of couples, they have never, from the beginning of their relationship, sat down together and spoken about their individual values and beliefs, or what is important to each of them.

Most, when they decide to commit to each other, either by moving in and living together, having a civil partnership or marriage commitment or having children, haven't even spoken about the way they see their future together, what roles they will take on within the relationship, or what their dreams and aspirations are; they just muddle through. A healthy relationship is one where the couple discuss their own individual wants and needs, and then work together as a team to meet both of their wants and needs.

Why communication is vital in any relationship is that we all have different understandings on things, therefore we should not assume we know what the other wants and needs, but we should ask them so we understand things from their perspective.

Once we ask, we should continue to ask, because we all change throughout time and we all have the ability to change our minds. Just because a course of action, or a type of supportive gesture, meets our wants and needs at some point, it doesn't mean it continually will. It's always best to touch base every now and again to see if you're both okay as individuals and that you are working as effectively as possible, as a couple, to ensure the relationship works.

The same really applies to roles within the relationship. Where are the conversations about who does what? Is it that we drift into stereotypical gender specific traditional roles, whereby the thinking is that the female does the homemaking and caring roles, whilst the male adopts the breadwinner and protective roles, and where does the stereotypical gender roles thinking fit into same sex relationships? Whether it makes sense to adopt such gender roles in this day and age is a different matter, but without a discussion, individuals can feel taken for granted, unappreciated, undervalued, feeling that their wings have been clipped and they are not living the life they want to.

All these things can either have a positive or negative effect on the emotional and psychological connection. If one partner feels unappreciated by their partner, then over a period of time this will have an adverse effect on the intimacy and sexual relationship of the couple. With some individuals, this lack of intimacy and sex will have an impact on the emotional and psychological element of their relationship, so it is important to talk about all of these things in order for resentments and blame not to be able to fester and take a hold.

210

Just take a moment to think about your own relationship, or ones that you have had in the past, where you have felt taken for granted and unappreciated etc. How has this impacted on not only you, but on your relationship?

There is no question that it will have had an effect, no matter how small or large. Now spare a thought for a victim where domestic violence is prevalent. What happens to the emotional connection when the partner is abusive, what happens where the abusive partner still wants intimacy or sex - how is that for the victim, how does that make the victim feel, and what happens when the perpetrator forces sex upon the victim, how do you think that would make the victim feel?

When there is sex without any intimacy or emotional connection, it makes me feel sick inside. With someone clambering on top of you, forcing their tongue inside your mouth, it doesn't resemble a picture of romance. You have this object forcing its way into your mouth and you're gagging out of pure panic. You feel as if you are choking and it's difficult to swallow. The hot breath on your face doesn't send a feeling of warmth shivering down your body out of passion, it makes you feel as if you are being smothered. When your partner forces their way inside you, you feel that your heart is turning into stone. You begin to switch off in order to deal with it, when suddenly you are brought back to reality by the pain inside you. You are not lubricated from any form of desire, so it stings like hell. You are just a piece of meat, there to satisfy your partner's wants and needs. They often have no desire to meet your wants and needs and they don't care how they get their own needs and wants met. Besides which, in their minds, how on earth would you ever find what they are doing to you repulsive and disgusting?

After reflecting on what's important and key for me in a relationship, it's the emotional connection that has to be in place first, then for the intimacy to follow and then for the sex after that. It's not to say that this way around is the way it has to be, as there have been occasions where there have been brief relationships or one night stands, where vital parts of the equation are missing. For me though, in order for a relationship to move forward, there needs to be that emotional connection.

There have been brief relationships in my life to date that I have ended because there is no emotional connection for me. It doesn't matter how good looking someone is. Yes, it's a turn on or a bonus, but it's not going to work for me if the emotional connection isn't there. If it is there, that's the element that needs to work continuously for me throughout the relationship, in order for that relationship to stay healthy and last.

Respect is another important element of a healthy relationship. I want a partner to value me and treat me with respect. If that is not there, or it was but something happens and it is lost, then without rebuilding that respect, then personally the relationship won't work for me.

Support is also key in any relationship, but especially in an intimate relationship. I want a partner to be there for me, to be by my side and to help where possible, to cover my back and to give me a hug when I've had a bad day, to wipe away the tears when I'm upset. When the weight of the world is on my shoulders, for them to help to share that burden and when I do something, they are, above all, proud of me.

Yes, even in the most difficult of relationships, you can get these things back, like respect, trust, support, love, intimacy and a connection, but it means that both partners have to be fully on board with it and work together at repairing the damage, and by both putting effort into the relationship to ensure the breakdown doesn't happen again.

In a relationship where these things are not present, or at least a number of them are not present, these are the warning signs, and when I have seen a lack of any of these things in a relationship since, I have either raised it as an issue for us to work on, both as individuals and as a couple, or I have broken off the relationship.

Getting back into the field of relationships was scary, because I was opening myself up to be vulnerable, and once I was vulnerable I was exposed. There was a constant shifting of the balance of being distant, cold or mysterious, to opening myself up and letting someone in enough, where there was then the potential for them to do some damage.

There were some individuals that I had a brief relationship with that I had no emotional connection with, where I thought "what the hell", but I knew these relationships were not going to last. They would just plug the gap of pain and hurt temporarily. There were individuals that I had a brief relationship with where there wasn't any kind of spark, it was going to be nice perhaps, but dull, and because there was no emotional connection I could end it without getting hurt. Of course, I was upset because it's not a nice thing to do to, ending a relationship with anyone, especially if they are more into you than you are of them, it's an unpleasant thing to do. It's almost as if it's a 'catch twenty two' situation: either have no emotional connection and I won't get hurt, or have an emotional connection and get hurt. Bizarre how emotions work sometimes, don't you think?

For a while, there were a couple of relationships that were more flings than anything else, because these individuals were attached. That seemed safe to me, and that's why I went for it. These relationships were intense and exciting, but they were never going to go anywhere. They were relationships that enabled me to open up a little, but the circumstances meant that I was never going to be exposed enough emotionally to get seriously hurt. In a way these relationships helped me on the road to recovery and enabled the healing process to take effect, because I felt wanted and special in a way, and yet if I stopped long enough to examine my thoughts and feelings, I also on the other hand felt a little undervalued. At the time though, the positives of these types of relationships far outweighed the negatives.

It's not something that I would ordinarily do, i.e. entering into a relationship with someone who was attached, because my natural character is to generally put other's feelings and needs first, but coming out of that violent and abusive relationship made me realise that I needed to begin to put myself first and ensure that my needs and wants were put first for a change, even if that was temporary or surrounded by a kind of falseness.

It seemed like it was something that I needed to get out of my system, rightly or wrongly, and I did just that. Perhaps to some that might seem selfish of me, but I needed to get to a point where I put me as a priority, and until I got to a point where I could regulate that new found philosophy to a healthier position or perspective, then of course there would be some collateral damage along the way.

It got to a point where it did regulate itself, and I got bored of the socialising and the brief relationships and flings, because I didn't need or want any of it anymore. I was happy in myself and at last felt content in my own skin. I felt confident with my own ability and where I had got to. I was proud of the work that I was doing, and I had got back to being fit and healthy.

Here's the thing though, when you're at that point where you no longer want or need someone else to make yourself happy and you stop looking, that's when, more often than not, the right person comes around and on that rare occasion when such an opportunity presents itself, it seems a massive waste if you don't throw caution to the wind and go with it. Just make sure if you do throw caution to the wind that you have a gigantic safety net underneath in case you fall or want to jump ship.

Someone did come into my life and they met nearly all the things on my list, if not everything, but these are things not to just tick off and say yes, those elements are met. There needs to be a constant effort to continue to reassess, discuss, renegotiate, plan and move forwards in the same direction. Otherwise you just drift apart and unless intervention and sacrifices are made, to ensure that you are on the same journey, then the gap sometimes becomes just a little too great.

The grass isn't always greener, but it's about sitting on that grass in the long run and ultimately being happy and content with yourself.

Chapter Ten

Falling Apart: When the world comes tumbling down

In an ideal world, life would run smoothly, meaning you have eventually found the happiness you so deserve, happiness within yourself, happiness in whatever you do and happiness with whoever you are with.

Then we wake up, because life isn't like that. It throws us lots of low curve-balls and sometimes we recognise them and are able to manoeuvre out of the way, sometimes we are equipped to deal with them, and sometimes those curve balls knock us over.

Life was great; I loved my work and managing to make a difference, I was confident within myself and with my ability and I had found happiness with someone special and then it hit - the realisation that I needed to leave my role as Domestic Violence Officer. I tried to block it out and to continue with my work but, as the days and months continued, it was much more difficult to stop it from having an effect or being able to manage it. It became difficult going into work every day, a place that had been my sanctuary; my lifeline, was no longer such a thing.

The environment began to affect my overall health and wellbeing. It's like when you work really hard at something, really focus and immerse yourself into it, and then you take time out to go on holiday, you get sick with a cold because you begin to relax a little, because you are not working at a constant high. The enormity of everything that had happened began to take its toll and this had an effect on my health. The only possible solution was a change of environment.

I moved to a unique role where there was only one officer carrying out that role, me! It was the role of Positive Action Officer and it would be challenging. It gave me the same autonomy as I had within the Domestic Violence Officer's role, and I gave it 100% of my attention, focus and ability and I began to make clear in-roads and began making changes in the right direction in order to make a difference.

The role of Positive Action Officer was created to make life in the police, whether as a police officer or as a member of the police staff, a level playing field for any employee from any under-represented minority group. It was also a role to encourage members of the public from minority groups to join the police force, either as police officers or police staff.

I faced a lot of resistance at first, from both within the police at all levels and also from community groups outside of the police, but I started making links with these groups and began to make strong connections. Within the police, I began to work with internal groups such as the Black Police Association, Women's Group, Disability Group, The Christian Police Association and was instrumental in setting up a Lesbian, Gay, Bisexual and Transgendered group.

It has always been important for me, in whatever role I have been in, to always ask the people things relate to for their ideas and their feedback, and it has always made sense to work with them as opposed to against them, and because of this I was able to begin to develop, implement and move forward key initiatives, projects, resources and action plans to make a difference and I found myself yet again in a privileged position of being able to influence guidelines and policies.

Unfortunately, operating at that level can come at a high price, perhaps a battle too far, or once too often putting my head above the parapet; it began to affect my health. I already had the physical issues through injuries during my police career, after being assaulted a number of times whilst on duty; these incidents resulted in lasting injuries to my shoulder, back and knee. This hindered and restricted my career in many ways, I managed the pain from these injuries through constant physiotherapy and eventually ended up needing surgical operations to try to limit the overall damage; a shoulder operation was successful in

220

removing pain, but I had a piece of collar bone removed and therefore my shoulder would restrict me from operational duties, which I hadn't realised prior to the operation. Even today the restricted mobility impacts on my life. I also had a knee operation, but again to this day there is still vulnerability with my knee and ongoing pain. My back however has been the most damaging of injuries, every morning after waking it takes an hour or so for my back to become free enough to move about, and sometimes everyday activities such as vacuuming or gardening, or even stepping off a kerb whilst walking, can set off several days where I have very restricted movement and debilitating pain, but whereas I could often manage the pain within the majority of my police career, I could not ultimately do anything with the restriction from the instability of the shoulder.

Now, there was also the emotional and psychological effect of everything that was now penetrating through my defensive barriers, of which I was at a loss to deal with. I didn't feel that I had the strength to deal with anything at that point in my life. I tried to ignore what was happening, I tried to tackle it head on and confront. Then I attempted to seek help through work and the appropriate informal channels, and finally there was no option but to take things through the formal route. The organisation was sorry for the impact, but was at a loss to deal with it.

It was too much for me at this time and, looking back at it now, my body began to react to the stress of it all. One night, my back seized up and it took me three hours to get out of bed and I ended up in hospital because of it. I went to my doctor's and was signed off for a few weeks. I couldn't cope any longer, it was too much and that's finally when I crumbled. Everything came crashing down and I went into meltdown emotionally, physically and psychologically.

I didn't get the space to think clearly. I would just spend days crying uncontrollably; I didn't want to venture out of the house and if the doorbell rang, even if it was just the Postman, I would just curl up on the floor in a corner where I couldn't be seen and cry. Senior managers came to see me to try to resolve the situation. They would apologise for the impact and try to look for a way to make things better, but again stated they were at a loss at how to deal with it. Whilst I was off, I was also told I was being moved from my role as Positive Action Officer and could go back to my former division in Harlow, so senior management did try to look for a way forward to get me back into work. Again they said sorry for what had happened but again they couldn't change it. Nothing worked because I was broken inside.

When I recognised that the apple of my eye, my partner, was rotten to the core, I could eventually leave and begin to work through the mess and chaos that was left of me and the situation and I could slowly rebuild my life by focusing on the one true thing that had always been so important to me: the police. It was the one true thing that had always been a pivotal point in my life; the only thing I had so strongly believed in and wanted more than anything else. I believed in the police from as far back as the age of seven, it was all I wanted to do. It was me through and through, and even now if you cut me in half there would be police officer in the middle.

Everything that I had believed in began to mist over and I couldn't make sense of any of it. I felt completely lost and alone. This time, I had no idea of how to cope and I was sinking, sinking fast. I therefore felt I had to process this fact and decide what to do with my future. I couldn't change things and, at that moment in time, I knew the only option I had was to ultimately leave the police. I had nothing left to fight with; I had nothing left at all.

I wrote my letter of resignation and as I did so the tears were streaming. I felt my life was definitely over; everything I had ever believed in was disintegrating before my very eyes. I'd been beaten. Something I swore to myself that, after leaving my violent and abusive partner, would never happen again happened. I had tried to confront it, I had tried to tackle it, but ultimately the only option for my health and wellbeing was to leave, and there started the point to which I fell completely into a big black dark hole.

Chapter Eleven

Black Hole: My Lowest Point

Everything not only seemed black and dark, it really was black and dark. It wasn't only a dark cloud hanging over me, I was engulfed by it; it was as if I was in a hole and couldn't get out. I was trying to climb out and I was also looking for someone to throw me a rope so I could get out, but nothing was working. I had to find my own way out of the dark place and that would mean working my way through the minefield of crap that life had thrown at me.

The pattern that I had experienced before with my violent and abusive partner seemed to be repeating itself; the issue had previously been my violent and abusive partner now the issue was the difficulties faced as a police officer. The difficulty of both was the experiences, the behaviour and the impact on my emotional, physical and psychological wellbeing; the course of action was the same for both: to ignore both behaviours, then try to tackle and confront it, but in the end the only option which had been left for both was for me to leave. I had left my violent and abusive partner and now I had to leave the police.

I left the police, moving to Cheshire to be closer to my family who still lived in north Wales and closer to the support network they provided. Both were circumstances that seemed enforced on me, of which neither did I want, yet in the end I made the decision to leave both, but still the impact and effects of leaving them caused a massive loss in my life. It was as if something had died and that something was me.

Being a police officer was who I was, it was someone I had always wanted to be, I was good at it and no one could ever say otherwise, I know that. I always gave 100% in whichever role I took on, on shift, within the Crime Desk, in additional specialist roles as a sexual offences officer, a family liaison officer, a grievance officer and ultimately for several years as the Domestic Violence Officer. Domestic violence is where I made the most difference, I had found my niche, I used my entire professional and personal experience and knowledge to provide a balanced approach to all things related to it, and that seemed to work.

I wouldn't change anything in my life within the police, I loved it and I loved the majority of the people I met and worked with. Being a police officer made me who I am today. I grew up in effect whilst being a police officer; I moved from being a child into an adult and Essex itself, and Essex police, will always have and hold a special place in my heart.

Even the events that led me to leave the police have made me into the person that I am today, but without them there is no doubt I would still be a police officer, and if I had been given the appropriate space to work through what had happened to me and been able to rebuild those broken and shattered pieces and perhaps come to terms with the missing ones, then again I would still be there. I am still proud to have been a police officer with Essex police and even now I am proud of the work that force does. I still have many friends within the force whom I will always be proud to call my friends.

However, that said, when loss hits though, it hits hard.

Leaving the police, I lost my identity; I knew who I was as a police officer. I had my core beliefs and values; being a police officer was me. Now I didn't know who I was, I was a nobody. I lost my confidence, my self-esteem and above all my worth. My coping strategies were not great, I turned to food again as a comfort and to alcohol to numb and blot out the pain and negativity and, as a way of protecting myself, I withdrew from the world and from loved ones.

My rock who had helped me heal and recover previously, my little dog, was getting frail and poorly, so there was no motivating force to get me out of the house, whereas before I needed to take her out for walks, but now she wasn't allowed to

227

go - vets orders - so we both used to stay in. I would just sit there, caught up in my own thoughts. Every once in a while, my little dog would catch my eye and she would run over and demand a hug, which I dutifully obliged, and sometimes that would be enough to break the trance I found myself in.

My loved ones couldn't lift me from the gulf of despair and I knew they were struggling too. It's not easy to be the ones standing by and watching a loved one crumble, trying to help, support and love them, but feeling helpless and despondent when your efforts don't succeed. All you can do is be there and support them in whatever way you can, in the hope that one day very soon something happens and you see your loved one emerging from this dark place and once again you see that sparkle back in their eyes, but until that time it is so hard and, in turn for them, it questions their relationship with you.

Slowly over time though, with the space to think, I began to work through and explore what skills and resources I had used to heal and recover from previous losses or difficult situations. I looked at how I managed after leaving my violent and abusive partner and how I dealt with all the emotions that left me so vulnerable. Work was a massive life saver at that time, but clearly my work as a police officer wasn't the solution, because this time it was the cause of my pain and vulnerability and I had left. So I began to once again look at what was fundamentally important to me. It was still about making a difference, as always through my working life, so that would have to be a starting point for me; additionally having the love and support from my loved ones and above all to be myself. Once again I began to rebuild what was important to me. But could I really make a difference outside of the police?

I had been able to make a huge difference within the context of domestic violence; it had become a niche and one that I was good at. I did have in my mind that when I retired from the police, when my time was up, that I could do something connected to or with domestic violence. It was just that I hadn't planned on ever leaving before my retirement age. So in essence I was having these conversations a little too prematurely - fourteen years prematurely!

I began to look at appropriate job vacancies within Cheshire and the North West of England, but they seemed few and far between, so initially I widened my search and a vacancy came up to apply for a domestic violence position two hours away from where I was living; distance didn't seem to matter, so I completed the application form, which in itself was daunting as I had been in the police for sixteen years and times had changed within the context of applying for jobs, but I submitted it and was invited for an interview. I was nervous, perhaps because I had a lot riding on it, in that I needed a job for my own self-esteem and for my confidence to be raised. It was so important for me to feel valued again.

It seemed to go okay and a couple of days later they called me, but unfortunately I had been unsuccessful. I felt like I had been kicked in the stomach, I felt sick, but the woman on the phone told me the only reason they had not chosen me was the fact that I lived two hours away and that they needed someone to live nearby as it was a managerial position and I would be called out and would need to respond to any issues. She told me not to change anything about the way I had presented myself in the interview, or throughout the process, and said their loss would definitely be someone else's gain. That in itself was for me really positive; it gave me confidence to continue to look for something else.

I found something a little closer to home, within an hour's drive from where I was living. It was a vacancy within a local authority council, as a Community Safety Officer for domestic violence, who not only had responsibility for domestic violence within the council, but who would also have responsibility for being the coordinator of that area's domestic violence partnership forum. Right up my street I thought, hypothetically speaking. I completed the application form and was invited for an interview. One thing I had learnt from the previous interview was that if I was closer I would have got the job, so I went in to this new interview believing in myself. I wasn't arrogant or over confident, I just thought: I'm going to be myself and if you don't want me for my experience, my knowledge and skill set then you are not the right people or the right job for me.

Strangely enough, I think I was more at ease than the three people on the interview panel. It was an extremely hot day and as soon as I went into the room, after shaking their hands and introductions, I asked whether I could take my suit jacket off. It seemed to throw them off guard, they were all sitting there sweating with the heat in their jackets and by me doing that they seemed to agree amongst themselves that they too would all take their jackets off. I was also offered a standard glass of water, which most people say no to, because they are so nervous in an interview, but I knew it would buy me some time to settle in ready for the interview to begin, so I said yes and one of the interviewers began to pour me a glass of water and at that moment it was clear that the person was more nervous than me, because their hand was shaking so much! Again this put me at ease.

The interview seemed to go okay and I was told I would hear within a couple of days, as they had a number of other candidates to interview. Later the next day, I received a telephone call from one of the people on the interview panel who told me that they would like to offer me the job and would I accept it? I thanked them for the call and news and asked if I could think about it and get back to them within the next hour with my decision. Crazy you might think, but I just wanted to buy myself some time to jump up and down and scream with joy, in private with my loved one. So that is what we did, we hugged each other, I screamed with joy and bang on the hour later, I telephoned the interviewer back and accepted the position. That night, we celebrated and I felt myself beginning to climb out of that hole, one tiny step at a time.

Three weeks later, I started the role and began, as you do with most new jobs, learning the ropes. I wanted to meet as many people as possible and find out about the role and how it connected with the key representatives from other agencies, so I started to build up the connections and began, based on my experience and knowledge not only as a police Domestic Violence Officer but also from being a chair of a domestic violence forum, looking at ways to enhance and improve things relating to domestic violence.

I didn't go in full steam ahead, I listened to others and included them in my ideas and my thoughts; I was able to offer a balanced view and perspective and also some ways forward, because a number of things that they had been having issues or difficulties with, I had already previously encountered before, so I was able to make key changes in order to make a difference.

232

One of the most fundamental differences was to review the way the domestic violence partnership forum was operating and submit proposals to change into two groups, one the 'practitioner implementation' group and the other the 'strategic decision making' group.

It was also vital to have key representatives from all relevant agencies involved, who were at the most appropriate levels within their own organisations, so there were quite a few raised eyebrows when I suggested the strategic group should have directors or assistant directors from those agencies, and managers or senior practitioners for the implementation group. So that's what happened, key relevant individuals formed both groups, and as a collective whole we were able to meet ten out of the government's eleven 'best value' performance indicators, with the final indicator well on track to being met, a rarity not only on a more local basis but also on a national basis.

I also began to invest in myself and began to increase and develop my academic ability. It's all very well accumulating a wealth of experience, knowledge and skill set internally within a police environment, but when you come out of the police, without qualifications you are deemed to have limited experience, apart from being put forward for jobs such as a security guard, store detective or bouncer - nice really, when you have spent so long putting your life on the line for your country and community and have been in a position able to make a difference to other people's lives, who have faced difficulties and turmoil. Not that there is anything wrong with being put forward for such jobs, but they were not jobs for me.

I began a number of programmes of academic study relating to Counselling, domestic violence and relationship difficulties, in order to utilise my experience built up to date. I didn't want to waste the knowledge, skills and experience that I had built up over the years and wanted to continue to help others in a more effective way, by pulling all my skill set together, but in a way that could also be formally recognised.

I met some amazing people, but once you begin to shine at something and you are able to make clear important differences, people take note of that; some are really pleased that you are making such a difference, but some feel their noses are being put out of joint and it becomes challenging. Generally, I'm all for a challenge, but I was still jaded from leaving the police, so I thought, "I don't want to be in this position."

A key learning point from my exit from the police was not to let such individuals affect my health again, physically, emotionally or psychologically. From experience, I decided to shortcut the turmoil, therefore the answer was to hand my notice in again, but a key difference for me, having learnt the hard way, was to have more control over the way things happened to the benefit of me. So I found another vacancy before doing this, I applied for it, was interviewed, was accepted for it and had the confirmation in my hand to that effect before handing in my notice.

On being asked why I was leaving, because I was doing such a good job, I explained my reasons in a balanced way and wished them well. Again I had met some amazing and wonderful people from working within that position, particularly within the organisations that made up the domestic abuse forum, people who have passion and dedication. I still link in and connect with many and some I will always have fond memories of and remain friends with.

My new role was with the organisation 'Relate', at Greater Manchester South. I became the manager of their domestic violence perpetrator programme, which was a voluntary programme, as they had been successful in applying for a funding bid to work with male perpetrators of domestic violence and also run a women's safety programme for their partners. There, I helped a small team to create, develop and implement a successful, forty week rolling block programme, which consisted of part individual work and part group work.

There was substantial resistance for such a programme to be in place at the beginning, because many organisations who

235

predominantly worked with victims of domestic violence had the mindset that any monies or initiatives should be directed towards victims. It was a difficult process, therefore, to begin to change such mindsets, to get to a point where we have a more holistic approach and work with all involved in domestic violence, otherwise we would all constantly just be trying to put a sticky plaster on a wound, as opposed to healing it and preventing it from happening again.

I knew from my experience of being a police officer that domestic violence could only be combated in some way, by both victim and perpetrator having resources and help, as well as children and any others affected, directly or indirectly.

The role, although a good one which gave me more insight and strings to my so called bow, also restricted me in many ways. It narrowed my ability to be creative and to make a difference on a wider scale, as I wanted to continue to grow and develop. I had made a promise to myself that if I felt I was unhappy, or not doing something that I loved, I would leave on my own terms and not leave things to develop into a difficulty. I therefore eventually took the decision to hand in my notice.

I decided to not only focus on training around domestic violence and consultancy work, but I wanted to focus on my Counselling profession and become more hands-on again.

Having gained academic qualifications, including a master's degree in relationship therapy, and becoming a psychotherapist, together with practical Counselling experience through the relationship specialists Relate at Manchester and then Cheshire and Merseyside, I set up my own private Counselling centre, which specialises in domestic violence and relationship difficulties.

Owning my own business would be tough and demanding, but it would enable me to grow and develop. There would be no one in a position to chip away or intimidate me, to prevent my passion from shining through. Finally I could just get on with my work and continue to make a real genuine difference.

When you take a step forward, it's often easy to get carried away by the excitement of it all, and while it's so important to recognise how far you have come, it is also so important to have your feet firmly on the ground and make sure the foundations are strong enough to weather the next storm, and the next storm was about to come. I was aware that it was coming though, and I guess that was the difference.

The storm would be the biggest blow that I would have to encounter and I knew that it would be the most difficult one that I emotionally would have had to deal with to date. I needed to plan for it and put things or measures in place to protect myself from the damage, or at least try to limit the damage, if that were at all possible.

The hypothetical storm was set on a course to inflict as much damage as possible, and with the potential to ultimately destroy the rock that was in its path. That rock was my rock.

My little dog, who had been right by my side for so long, who had kept me going throughout the most difficult of times, had developed a terminal disease. The vets were amazing and gave her the best care at every step. She was a little fighter, such a strong character and such a wonderful, good natured personality. She was a loyal and loving little dog and I knew her loss would break my heart.

What I had learnt from all the previous difficulties in my life, and the different types of losses that I had encountered, was that I had built up my own ways of dealing with these in order to get through, but I had got through no matter what life had thrown at me. I had got through. It was painful, very painful and I often emerged with wounds and scars, but they eventually either sealed themselves or they actually healed.

The temptation was to run, but I couldn't run because she was still here, and it was my responsibility to look after her, as it always had been. She had always been there for me and I was always going to be there for her. The realisation that she wouldn't always be there was horrible, but even more traumatic would be the fact that she would deteriorate in front of my very eyes. Some people said to me, maybe I should step in and have her put down. What!

Would it have been easier to run away, and to have taken that route so early on, I doubt it, but anyway there was no way I was going to do that, the vets said there was no reason to do so, because she was so healthy and strong in herself to be able to live actively for some time, and above all she wasn't in any pain initially, so we would manage it. There were months when you wouldn't even know she was poorly, she would run up and down the garden full of beans, she would dribble her football around the garden, and I could see in her eyes that she was still so aware of her surroundings and everybody, but I knew the time would come. It was almost like a train crash waiting to happen.

I didn't know when the train was expected, so I kept looking along the track; I was looking for signs that it was there and sometimes there were false alarms. When I first saw it emerge around the corner in the far distance, I questioned myself as to whether it was there or not and then, as I tried to focus, it became clearer. It was heading towards us. Time seemed to be in slow motion and there was nothing that I could put in its way to stop it coming. The vets tried with tablets, but it just slowed the train down; it was still heading towards us. All I could do was to try and rationalise my thoughts, was she still okay, was she suffering, was I keeping her here because of me, was I keeping her here because she still had life in her? It was perhaps all of those things.

There was never ever going to be a right move or right time. The ultimate decision was always going to be difficult one. In myself, I knew when the time came, because it was when the sparkle seemed to disappear and she was no longer active or in control, and that was the time. It would be so difficult for me, but it was right for her which was more important. The vet was amazing; she was so very kind and thoughtful, carrying out the procedure in the most sensitive of ways.

Leaving my little rock alone in the vet's surgery that day, was possible the hardest thing I'd ever done in my life. More difficult than leaving my relationship, more difficult than leaving the police and I wouldn't be able to settle until I had her back with me so she wouldn't be alone.

Two days later, I got the call to pick up my little rock. I had been pacing up and down and I was sure there were no more tears that could possibly ever come out of my eyes ever again. I was wrong; the tears were there constantly for the weeks and months ahead. I decided to not keep my thoughts inside, but to write

240

them down daily or several times a day, so whenever I felt upset or low, I would write something; it was as if I was telling my thoughts to my little rock, like I would if she was next to me. I carried on doing that until there were no longer tears of sadness, but there were fond thoughts of the memories and times we had shared.

She was my rock and will always remain my rock.

What I realised was that you might physically lose something or someone, who plays such an important part in your life, and regardless of whether there are good times or bad, the memories are there if you look hard enough for them, because the ones that matter are there with you emotionally and psychologically. There will, of course, be times when naturally you think of them and there will be times when there will be a trigger that sets off your thoughts, feelings and actions when you least expect them to, but it's about utilising the experience, knowledge and skills that have worked for you in the past, in order to move forward and work your way through such loss.

Chapter Twelve

Making a difference today: Keeping my passion alive

Making a difference has always been my overall main aim in life and, corny as that may sound, it is the truth. Over the years, it has become more poignant the more I became aware that: if fate hadn't intervened so drastically with the losses of my parents' previous children; I was two months premature and might not have survived; I was in potentially dangerous and life threatening situations from being a police officer to being in a violent and abusive relationship; then I wouldn't actually be here.

There seems to be something keeping me here and I believe that is 'to make a difference'. Not only for me to make a difference in other peoples' lives, but more importantly for me to make my difference in the world, in order to justify my existence and prove something to myself: that being here is worth it!

I want to continue to move forward and continue to see, identify and to plug those gaps, not only in services and awareness, but for injustice and inequality. I have spent fourteen plus years delivering training around domestic violence and relationship difficulties, writing tailor-made domestic violence and relationship difficulties programmes, for a wide range of organisations or agencies, both whilst within the police and outside, and it is important for me to continue to raise awareness and educate others around the issues and complexities of domestic violence and the impact and effect it has, both short and long term, for all involved.

You can keep up to date with my comments and views by visiting my website **www.tinaroyles.com** where I share information through blogs and other means.

I also regularly appear in the media, on a local, national and international basis, regarding domestic violence and relationship challenges, commenting not only on the subject matter, but on celebrity and high profile cases and likewise some of these may feature on the above website.

As mentioned in the previous chapter, I am a psychotherapist and own and operate a private Counselling practice, which specialises in domestic violence and relationship difficulties and challenges.

Here I work with clients who have been victims of domestic violence and provide an environment to explore change and recovery. I also work with clients who have not only been perpetrators of domestic violence, but clients who have anger management difficulties which impact on their relationships. I also work with individuals and couples who want relationship Counselling.

For information on Counselling sessions with me, please visit the following website **www.selyortherapycentre.com** and for those of you thinking what a strange name for a therapy centre, it is actually my surname backwards; my grandfather (my dad's father) owned a shop before I was born called Selyor Stores, so I thought it only fitting to continue the tradition.

I have provided some information in the appendices on why we should intervene in domestic violence and also the seven key tips if someone you know is experiencing domestic violence.

On my website **www.tinaroyles.com** there will be blogs that link to portable document format (PDFs) and also links to digital audio encoding formats (MP3s) through a variety of means, which again will enable me to share information with you.

There are many 'frequently asked questions' relating to domestic violence and some perhaps I will have answered for you within this book through my experiences, others I continually answer on my website blogs.

I want to touch base again briefly on some of my own questions that I have raised around my life and experiences, and domestic violence, and answer them in the simplest of forms, although these questions will deserve more of my attention in the future, to investigate further, to explain myself. For example:

Q: Did I think the way I thought about loss or dealt with loss kept me in the domestic violence relationship?

A: Yes it was certainly an aggravating factor.

Q: Did my lack of confidence and my own lack of self-belief hinder my decision to leave and stay somewhere I shouldn't have stayed?

A: Yes of course it played a part.

Q: In relation to dealing with difficult situations or individuals, did my lack of ability to handle them play a part in keeping me in the relationships, or in difficult positions, throughout my life?

A: Yes it was an aggravating factor.

Q: Did limited finances and lack of perceived resources stop me from leaving sooner?

A: Of course they did.

Q: Did the fear of how others would perceive me or judge me play a part?

A: Definitely.

Q: Overall, was it the fact I thought I wouldn't be able to cope that kept me in a vulnerable place?

A: Certainly.

All of these things made a difference. Relationships in general are complex, and where there is domestic violence there is no question that it is very complex and chaotic, and you need as much help and support as possible, so that when even the smallest opportunity arises, you are ready to take that opportunity while you can.

Domestic violence destroys the lives of those directly involved and changes lives forever, in some way, by the scars it leaves. Not solely the physical reminders, but the emotional and psychological ones deeply embedded.

For every moment you stay in such a relationship, the violence and abuse eats away at you, piece by piece, until there is nothing left of you. You look at your reflection and you are a shadow of your former self. In fact you are a ghost.

If you leave, you will be able, over time, to rebuild some of those broken and damaged pieces, either on your own or through appropriate support and help. Help is out there, but it is essential to ensure that, if you seek professional help, they are experienced and have in-depth knowledge of the nature and complexities of domestic violence, in order for them to provide a safe environment to explore and to enable a platform from which you can start to recover and heal.

If these pieces are left broken and damaged, they will continue throughout your life to cause you harm and in effect they have the potential to become the ticking time bomb inside you. Leaving a domestic violence relationship, or when you are thinking of leaving, heightens the risk of danger and vulnerability.

It is vital and paramount that you seek help to protect yourself and any children. When safe to do so take action, reach out and get the help and support you deserve. With appropriate help and support, and above all the safety measures in place, you can begin to move forward, to rebuild your life, recover and heal from the impact.

Don't let the impact and effects of domestic violence destroy or kill you or someone that you love.

Appendix 1

Why should we as a society intervene in domestic violence?

Domestic Violence is such a complex issue; there is no one reason why it happens. There may be aggravating factors such as alcohol, drugs, financial worries, work pressures, arguments over children and everyday stresses and strains.

As a society, we cannot give one exact reason as to why domestic violence happens and, because of this, it is therefore difficult to stop, because one size does not fit all.

This is why I do not think that we will ever stop the very first incident of domestic violence from occurring in a relationship. What we therefore need to do is to try to work together to stop the number of repeat incidents involving the same people.

We could do this by all agencies, whether statutory, private, voluntary, charitable, and society as a whole, dealing with it positively and treating it seriously for all involved, directly or indirectly, when faced with it.

It is often all too easy for some agencies and elements of society to try to label the behaviour, because we don't like it when we don't have a reason why, but by continually trying to narrow it down to specific reasons, or ideas, we neglect other aspects. An example of my thinking is when research is conducted to look at any links or connections between domestic violence and mental health, then money gets diverted to projects or initiatives around this and as a result some agencies and groups focus their attention on this issue; also when there is research presented around any links or connections between domestic violence and alcohol, again money gets diverted to projects or initiatives around this and as a result some agencies and groups focus their attention on this issue. There is a constant shift of focus and, as a result of this shift, other projects and initiatives are affected or close down.

Not everyone who has a drink goes and assaults their partner.
Not everyone who has pressure at work or financial worries goes and assaults their partner.

THESE ARE GENERALLY JUST EXCUSES.

SELF ESTEEM

Self-esteem plays a very important part in the issue of domestic violence; how people think and feel can affect the possible way in which they react to the circumstances that they find themselves involved in.

EXAMPLE

When you are at work and your boss comes in to see you and tells you that they are really pleased with the work you have done recently and that you are a credit to the company, how would that make you feel?

ANSWER

You will feel really proud of yourself, you will be happy that your work has been noticed, you will feel valued and respected, and it will improve your enthusiasm and your confidence.

EXAMPLE

How would you feel if you are at work and your boss comes in to see you, they tell you that you are under performing, that your work has suddenly become shoddy, your colleagues have told them that you don't appear to be making an effort and that you are not taking pride in your appearance anymore, how would that make you feel?

ANSWER

You will feel rejected, you will feel undervalued, you will feel hurt, your self-confidence will plummet, you will feel let down by your friends that you thought you could trust; it might make you uncomfortable in that environment in the future.

VICTIMS OF DOMESTIC VIOLENCE

Now think of the victim/survivor of domestic violence who is told, not once but constantly, by the person that they love that:

- They are useless.
- That they cannot do anything right.
- They have nothing important to say.
- That if their partner didn't want them no one else would want them.
- That they look plain, don't dress nice anymore, they have put weight on and are fat.
- That they are a bad parent.

Think for a minute… if you were in that person's shoes, how would that make you feel?

- Your self-esteem would be affected; your confidence would hit rock bottom.
- After a time, you would start to believe that what your partner is saying is true
- You would question your ability in every area.
- You would become withdrawn and you would start to feel worthless.

- You would become vulnerable.

REASONS WHY VICTIMS STAY

- Sometimes it's because the violence and the arguments don't happen all of the time and, when it isn't happening, things between them might be good, and that ultimately they love their partner.
- Sometimes it is because of the fear of the unknown, that they are scared to leave, where will they go, how they will manage?
- There may be financial reasons to stay; they may have a nice house and a nice circle of joint friends. Do they really want to lose that?
- They may stay through fear that no one will believe them.
- If they have children, what affect will it have on them, taking them away from their father/mother … In the victim/survivor's eyes, the offender has never hit the children.

WHY DO SOME VICTIMS LEAVE?

- They have had enough of the abuse.
- Because they are scared that next time the injuries could be worse or even fatal.
- Because of the effect that it's having on the children.
- They want to get on and have a better life.

- They have help and support from friends, family and other agencies.

WHY DO SOME VICTIMS GO BACK?

Why do some victims, once they have found the courage to leave, then go back?

- Because they love their partner.
- Because they think that they can help their partner.
- Because there is nowhere for them to go.
- They may be offered a Refuge space - but they might not be used to that environment, so therefore go back home.
- Due to the children missing the offender.
- Due to pressures from family and friends.
- Through lack of help and support from some agencies
- From not being believed.
- As their self-esteem and confidence is low, they may find that they cannot cope on their own, due to the power and control over them by their partner; they have learnt to become dependent on their partner and may feel isolated and lost without them.

GOING TO THE POLICE

There are some professions that will always have an effect on some people.

EXAMPLE

When a person, who is normally confident, knows what they want and have the ability to put their point across, is faced with meeting their bank manager, why then do they become a jittering wreck?

Why for example, if a law abiding member of the public is stopped by the police, when they get back into their car, why does he or she stick their car into reverse and drive towards the police car parked behind them - rather than stick it into first gear and drive forward. Why, after being stopped, do they then pull out in front of oncoming traffic rather than look first?

Why do some people, when dealing with their child's teacher, suddenly become overwhelmed and unable to hold a sensible discussion?

ANSWER

Because all of us can feel intimidated by what we have learnt over the years.

With this in mind:
- Put yourself in the place of the victim/survivor;
- Who may have been assaulted numerous times (currently average statistics state 37 previous times);

- Who finds the courage and is brave enough to walk into the Police Station or phones the Police for help;

- Bearing in mind that their self-esteem is low, that they are used to being criticised, that they have been told by their partner that no one will believe them - especially the authorities - it might be the first time that they are seeking help - think how frightened and scared they must be feeling.

BODY LANGUAGE

They have been used to their partner's body language, i.e. mocking them, criticising them and not respecting them.

They will pick up on the officer's behaviour and body language. Does the Officer believe the victim/survivor. This will be important to them.

The victim/survivor provides a statement to Police; they are re-living what has happened to them.

The victim/survivor is used to playing down the violence in their mind in order for them to deal with it and carry on. Therefore they will be used to minimising the importance of the situation - this may come across when giving details.

To the officer the victim/survivor may not appear as scared as they would expect/presume. But this is because the victim/survivor has got used to it. It may be that the victim/survivor has switched off their emotions in order to carry on.

After the offender gets arrested, he/she may be given bail conditions to stay away. Does the offender listen and stay away? Or does the offender contact the victim/survivor and get them to change their mind, promising the victim/survivor that they have learnt their lesson, that they will get help? Or saying if the victim/survivor continues with the complaint, it will split them up, and the victim/survivor may lose everything, that they can sort things out themselves, that they shouldn't be having other people poke their nose into their affairs?

The offender will have control over the victim/survivor; physically, emotionally and psychologically.

Will the victim/survivor drop the complaint or will they tell police that the offender has broken their conditions? It will take the victim /survivor a lot of courage to do the latter.

COURT

- If it gets to court what will happen?
- Will the victim/survivor be strong enough to turn up and give evidence?

EVEN WITNESSES UNDER NORMAL CIRCUMSTANCES ARE AFRAID OF ATTENDING AND GIVING EVIDENCE AT COURT!

However, here you would have a vulnerable person giving evidence against the person that they love, the person who has inflicted physical, emotional and mental abuse on them...

A PERSON WHO HAS POWER AND CONTROL OVER THEM.

- Who knows what buttons to press and who knows the victims/survivors weaknesses!
- The victim/survivor will be aware of the offender's body language in the court, the way they look at them; the victim/survivor will know what that look in the offender's eye means ...

BECAUSE THE VICTIM/SURVIVOR WILL HAVE SEEN IT MANY TIMES... THE LOOK THAT SAYS: JUST YOU WAIT.

The victim/survivor is being questioned by a trained professional about their relationship, about whether they are telling the truth; they will be interrogated to all intents and purposes.

THIS WILL BE A FRIGHTENING EXPERIENCE FOR THEM... ONE THAT MAY OVERWHELM THEM!

- After giving their evidence - what will happen?
- Will the offender be punished for their actions, or will they get off lightly?!
- If they get off lightly, how will that make the victim/survivor feel?
- Will they feel that what has happened to them has been treated seriously...?
- On the other hand, will they feel let down?!
- Will they be willing to report it if it happens again?
- Or will they not have faith or belief in the authorities?

REMEMBER - DOMESTIC VIOLENCE IS A CRIME AGAINST HUMANITY - WE MUST TREAT IT SERIOUSLY

Victims/survivors learn to minimize the violence in their minds, so that what has happened to them does not seem as bad to them.

People who work within agencies and authorities that deal with domestic violence get used to hearing similar cases everyday... it is important that they do not get blasé about what they hear.

THE SITUATION IS VERY REAL TO THE VICTIMS/SURVIVORS OF DOMESTIC VIOLENCE AND HAS A HUGE IMPACT ON THEIR LIVES.

SOME EMOTIONAL REACTIONS TO VIOLENCE MIGHT BE:

- THE NUMBING OF EMOTIONS
- TRIVIALISING VIOLENCE
- FREQUENT ILLNESSES
- FEELING RESPONSIBLE FOR THE ABUSE
- WITHDRAWING INTO ONE`S SELF
- ANGER ABOUT THE VIOLENCE/ CHAOS
- EMBARRASSMENT
- FEARS
- DEPRESSION

ABUSIVE RELATIONSHIP

Apart from the violence, how would you know if you were in an abusive relationship?

Things to consider -

1. Does your partner expect/insist on detailed reports of your daily activities?

2. Do you question your ability to do tasks you used to do easily and very well?

3. Do you feel you cannot live without your partner?

4.   Does your partner tell you that no one else will want you?

5.   Does your partner call you names?

6.   Does your partner ridicule/insult your family and friends?

7.   Do you feel uneasy being with your partner and your friends at the same time for fear of a scene?

8.   Do you often feel you're walking on eggshells?

9.   Does your partner threaten to "punish you?"

10.   Does your partner ridicule you for crying or worrying?

11.   Are you afraid no one else would like the 'real you?

The information in the bullet point list above has been used many times by many agencies/individuals over the last 15-20 years and the original source is unknown. However one good resource for up to date statistics and data is the Home Office Website: ***https://www.gov.uk/domestic-violence-and-abuse***

When someone tells you that they are a victim of domestic violence... be aware, listen to what is being said... and I mean really listen!

When you hear that the offender has dragged the victim about but there are no marks... remember how terrifying that could be for the victim!

When you hear the offender has placed their hands around the victim's throat, but there are no marks, think how scared the victim must have felt!

When the victim says, "they shouted at me," think how scared the victim must have been!

When you hear that the offender was verbally abusive, think about the impact and the real effect those words would have on the victim. How would you feel?! Think about the intimidation, the invading of personal space, what was the offender's intention, did they know that their actions or words would scare the victim? Think of not only the physical injuries, but the emotional and mental abuse that is being inflicted too!

Think about the offender saying that it was an accident, that they just lost control! Why don't they just lose control then when they have just had an argument with their mates in the pub?! Why do they just lose it with their partner?

Why if the victim goes to work, does the offender inflict injuries that cannot be seen, that can be covered up by clothing? Because the offender still wants the victim to go out and earn money. The offender is in control of their actions.

If the offender has inflicted injuries that can be seen: think about why. Is the offender jealous of the victim going to work? Is the intention to stop the victim from going through embarrassment? Is it to stop the victim from socialising with their family and friends? Think about it!

REMEMBER DOMESTIC VIOLENCE: Is a power and control issue - please don't underestimate it!

VICTIMS' RIGHTS

- Victims have the right NOT to be responsible for their partner's problems.
- Victims have the right to say NO.
- Victims HAVE the right to have their own opinions, to express them and to be taken seriously.
- Victims have the right to earn and control their own money.
- Victims have the RIGHT to be SAFE.
- Victims have the RIGHT to be treated with RESPECT.

REMEMBER

- Anyone can be a victim of domestic violence.
- Victims die each and every week from domestic violence incidents.
- Domestic violence is a social issue that needs to be dealt with.

- Family, friends, colleagues, neighbours, agencies, authorities, employers, all need to help support victims of domestic violence; raise awareness and assist in the campaign to stamp out such a social and complex issue!

SAME SEX RELATIONSHIPS

How does everything already mentioned relate to those suffering domestic violence in a same sex relationship? All of it applies!

However there are additional issues as well:
- Isolation.
- Privacy.
- "Not out" to family, friends and work colleagues.
- Fear of authority – myth that authorities will treat them badly.
- Fear that their partner will leave them. In some cases, there may only be that partner in their lives – they may have been cut off by everyone else due to their sexual orientation.
- They may not have come to terms with their own sexual orientation yet, therefore they may be embarrassed to report anything.
- Fear of people finding out about their sexual orientation.
- Fear of losing their job.
- Threats made by their partner to 'out' them, to inform family, friends, work colleagues and agencies that they are

lesbian, gay, bisexual or transgendered – to "out" them
without their permission (homophobic control)

ISSUES FACING THE POLICE

Domestic violence is very complex and difficult to deal with
anyway. Issues facing the Police are:

Lack of awareness of Police Officers and other agencies in
dealing with same sex issues.

Officers may not realise that the incident is a domestic incident,
i.e. not aware that the two persons in front of them are a couple
or have been in a relationship – parties may not disclose the fact
that they are gay.

Unwillingness of victim to cooperate with the investigation or
prosecution.

Victim's fear of authorities based on media coverage; concern
that they will refuse to help, that they will excuse or deny the
seriousness of the violence.

Concerns about revealing their sexual orientation to service
providers, family, friends or colleagues.

264

Improved training for Police is required – with the need to address homophobia and discrimination within that organisation. To develop written and spoken language in policies and literature that is inclusive of the LGBT community.

OTHER GROUPS

BLACK MINORITY ETHNIC (BME)

There are the additional issues of forced marriages, extended families living together; there may be a language barrier for seeking help, there may be transport issues to seek help, there may be fear of authorities or agencies. I have been told on many occasions by victim/survivors of domestic violence that are from third world countries, that the police are to be feared, due to the violence and aggression they show. It is therefore very hard to break this view point in relation to our own police officers. But again police officer training should highlight these issues/concerns. Raising awareness and doing campaigns should highlight these issues/concerns and seek to re-address these impressions.

MALES

Males are victims of domestic violence also. It is something that is rarely highlighted, but it goes on. It isn't a new thing, it has been happening for as long as it has been happening to women. I have dealt with many men who have been assaulted by women.

Their reasons for not reporting previous incidents to police or other agencies are again: fear of not being believed, false counter allegations, etc. Again good training on awareness for officers should highlight best practice. There is also a fear of peer pressure, what would their friends and family think? And the fear having no one to talk to about their circumstances. Up until the last few years, there were very few agencies that had or made provisions for male victims and very few refuges for male victims.

ELDERLY/VULNERABLE

This is an issue that has only in the last five years been highlighted, and again the awareness is not adequate.

Who protects the victims from a relative or one who is appointed as their Carer ?

Who takes the time to listen when an elderly or vulnerable person tells you they have bruises, that they are being shouted at, that they are being manhandled? General perception was "they're frail" or "they bruise easily" or "they may be difficult" or "how does the Carer manage?"

Due to these perceptions, issues such as domestic violence were allowed to go on unnoticed.

Who takes notice? The generation we live in today – how many of us pop in for chats with our neighbours like our grandparents did? How many of us check to see if our neighbours are okay, if we haven't seen them for a while? If anyone did call round and saw a bruise thought, "they must have fallen over," who then questioned or challenged?

There is work being done to highlight the issues of the elderly/vulnerable in relation to domestic violence, by Age Concern and other agencies, and in particular the organisation Elder Abuse.

The awareness of the general public however is very low, and needs to be highlighted on a large scale.

CHILDREN
Children are victims of domestic violence, whether directly or indirectly. There have been great improvements over the last five years in the services and organisations available in helping children. There has also, through the introduction of the citizenship curriculum in schools, been the opportunity to take the issues of domestic violence, peer pressure, relationships, etc. into the schools and raise the awareness of the school children. There has also been the training given to staff within the schools on domestic violence. Awareness via the media is prominent, but needs to remain constant.

ANIMALS

Pets can and are often used in domestic violence cases, whether injury is inflicted on them also, or using threats to hurt them, kidnap them, or destroying them, as emotional control over a victim/survivor. The RSPCA has highlighted this in studies conducted. I can also confirm many victims have highlighted this to me over the years. There are a number of organisations and charities involved with animals that are aware of the impact of domestic violence and have taken this into account through the services they offer. However, there are still many organisations which are not aware of the link between domestic violence and animal abuse.

THE WAY FORWARD

Despite the increase in awareness on domestic violence, there are still horrific cases which slip through the net and each and every one of us must be vigilant.

Issues are generally only topics on agendas for short spaces of time, and unless awareness is continually raised and highlighted, people lose interest and slip back into old ways of not getting involved, thinking - why should I get involved, it doesn't affect me, so why should I help?

Domestic violence affects everyone in society, whether directly or indirectly, it is a huge social issue/concern.

268

At present, it relates to a quarter of all reported crime and bear in mind not everyone reports domestic violence, if they did the figures would be unthinkable.

Domestic violence has long term effects on all those involved; the effects stay with the victim even if they have left the offender.

Workplaces need to have as standard, human resource (HR) good practice and policies on domestic violence, provisions put in place in other policies such as sickness or absence policies for consideration of the issues.

Training should be given to the human resource/employee relations department, on the subject of domestic violence, how this affects its employees, as victims or as offenders.

Training and awareness should then be rolled out to other staff. Support and welfare needs to be provided for the employees suffering from domestic violence.

Why this assistance? – Absence levels are high in most organisations, victims don't generally come out and say they are off due to domestic violence, other ailments are given; if they have injuries – how many of them will just say they fell over?

If the organisation had a good clear policy, had raised awareness and welfare and support was good – then victims may feel strong enough and confident enough to seek help from their employer.

If commitment, loyalty and assistance are given to the employee, then there would be increased morale, loyalty, commitment and productivity by the employee. Therefore addressing the issue of domestic violence would not only help the employee, but also the employer.

Intervention should be taken into account on moral grounds and from a human resource perspective; however, if not, there is also the cost benefit for employers via preventing absence.

Raising the awareness must continue, to organisations, agencies and to the general public.

Training must be undertaken by organisations and agencies in relation to domestic violence.

Initiatives must continue to be undertaken on the subject of domestic violence.

Everyone must strive to make domestic violence a social issue, and an issue that isn't tolerated in our society.

AGENCIES AVAILABLE

There are many agencies, on a national and a local level, available to help with the issues surrounding domestic violence. A way to find them is either by way of your local directory (at the front of the directory under useful numbers or under such headings as support groups), by leaflets from your local council, or via the internet. Also via approaching a key agency that has a statutory duty, imposed by the Crime and Disorder Act, to be involved in partnership work with other agencies – these key statutory agencies are police, social services and the council.

Each of these agencies will have representatives on domestic violence groups/forums/crime and disorder groups and will have strong links with other agencies, both voluntary and statutory.

Other key agencies involved with domestic violence are:

- Victim Support Scheme (VSS)
- Women's Aid
- Social Services Family Services Team
- Social Services Elderly Team
- Health Authority
- Child Protection Team
- Home Start
- Relate
- Age Concern

- Careline
- Family Mediation Services
- Police Domestic Violence Units
- Police Child Protection Units
- Police Hate Crime, Race, and Vulnerable Minority Teams
- Solicitors – Family and Domestic Violence Solicitors
- Probation Service
- Alcohol and Drug Advisory Service (ADAS)
- Mental Health Units
- Citizen's Advice Bureau
- National Society Prevention of Cruelty to Children (NSPCC)
- Child line
- Samaritans

There are many other agencies involved on a local basis to assist.

Appendix 2

7 Key Tips: If someone you know tells you they are experiencing domestic violence

1. Safety is paramount: help them with any safety planning.
2. Listen to them.
3. Tell them you believe them.
4. Offer them support.
5. Do not lay blame.
6. Do not judge them.
7. Avoid Saying

When talking about domestic violence and abuse, it can often become confusing when referring to individuals as the abused party or the abuser, there are also different connotations from using the term 'victim', as some individuals who have experienced or who are experiencing domestic violence and abuse do not see themselves as a victim and yet others prefer to use the term 'victim'.

On the other hand, some individuals prefer the term 'survivor', as they feel that they have survived the violence and abuse on a daily basis, and they gain strength from that term, others do not like the term 'survivor', as even if perhaps they have left the violent or abusive relationship, they still feel trapped in the emotions and memories triggered.

It is also important to recognise that domestic violence and abuse can happen to anyone, regardless of their gender or sexuality; statistics that are available state domestic violence and abuse affects more women than men, therefore the majority of literature, education and resources are tailored with this in mind. My aim is not to exclude someone from receiving the help and advice that they might need, so I will use non-specific gender names to identify the abuser and the abused.

The abuser/perpetrator of the violence and abuse will be identified as Sam.

The abused/victim/survivor of the violence and abuse will be identified as Chris.

1.   Safety is paramount – Help them with any safety planning

Those experiencing domestic violence will often play down or minimise the danger that they face on a continual basis in order to `normalise` the situation and be able to cope with their daily life. Whether Chris indicates that they want to stay in the relationship or whether they want to make steps to leave their

274

partner (Sam), whether the abuse or violence is inflicted by a close family member (Sam), or whether the abuse or violence comes from an ex-partner (Sam) who won't let go, their safety is the most important thing.

If Chris, any children or anyone else (including pets) are in any immediate danger, then calling the police should be a primary consideration.

Another option would be to take Chris to a place of safety in order for them to consider their options.

If Chris is not in immediate danger, then you could help them write down their own personal safety plan; this is a written plan of instructions on what to do if Sam threatens, expresses or follows through with any violence or abuse, as if this happens then Chris will not be in a position to think clearly enough in that situation and may need to have prepared a plan which they have read over and over again so it is clearer in their mind.

The plan should also contain a list of things to take with them, such as: any personal legal documents, including passport, birth certificate, any marriage or civil partnership certificate, bank details, National Insurance Card/Number, National Health Medical Record Card/Number, any documents relating to any benefits that may be in place, driving licence and any vehicle documents (Vehicle Excise Licence, MOT Certificate, and Insurance details); if there are any children, it is important not to forget any documents relating to them on the list: birth certificates, custody/access details, National Health Medical Record Card/Number.

It is also vital that Chris is able to put aside some money, as they may need to have emergency money for a variety of things such as access to a pay phone, if they leave the house and need to call for help, or might need to pay for a taxi/bus, pay for any food or toiletries, or accommodation if they leave in a hurry.

It is also important to take any medication that they use/need with them, including any medication that any children need also.

So, as you can see, the list can be lengthy, therefore unless thought through something may be left behind which could pose difficulties later on.

It is also important to remember important sentimental items, as these may be damaged or destroyed by Sam if they are not taken. It is also vital to take any sentimental items that the children have also, such as their favourite toy, their comfort blanket or their favourite clothes.

It may be that you would be in a position to store a suitcase or bag for Chris, in order for them to keep some, if not all, of the items above, especially if they are just thinking about leaving or whether leaving the relationship is imminent.

For more information regarding safety planning, why not visit the website **www.tinaroyles.com** and download the free 21 page information pack on services relating to domestic violence.

2.   Listen to them

Those that have experienced, or are experiencing, domestic violence and abuse, may not have had anyone whom they could talk to or confide in, therefore you might be the first person that they have told, or if they have told others, they may not have been taken seriously and may not have been listened to.

Therefore, it is vital that you take the time to listen to them, and I mean really listen to them. If you are not open to listening to Chris or taking the time to speak with them, then they may never open up or ask for help again. This happens, and when it does Chris might feel they have no one to turn to and either stay in an abusive relationship with Sam, and/or may turn to a variety of coping mechanisms such as alcohol, drugs, gambling or may even turn to crime, such as shoplifting, violence against others or prostitution as a way of crying out for help; others may feel so desperate that they feel they cannot cope or go on and may attempt to, as a cry for help, or follow through with thoughts of suicide. It is therefore vital that you take the time to listen to someone in a domestic violence situation.

It would also be important for Chris to see and hear that you are listening; if they pick up on the fact that you are not, then again they will close down and not tell you, or anyone else, again what they are or have experienced.

Think about how you actually listen to others; we live in such a busy often hectic world, where we are often thinking of several things at once and are trying to balance everything. Do we really have or make time for others? When someone is talking to you, do you give them your full attention or, if you were being completely truthful with yourself, what percentage of your full time and attention do you think you give them?... think about it for a moment.

What do you do, in order to let the other person know you are listening? For example:

Do you nod as if acknowledging what they have said, or as a way of encouraging them to continue with their conversation?

Do you keep eye contact with them to show that you are fully engaged, or do your eyes wander to what is happening or going on around them?

Do you let them say what they want to say or feel able to say, or do you interrupt them, or try to finish their sentences for them?

Do you paraphrase or summarise what they say, in order to gain clarity and to show them that you have been listening?

Listening to someone who has experienced, or is experiencing, domestic violence and abuse is an important step in the process of them getting or seeking help.

3. Tell them you believe them

What is important to highlight here is that abusers can often be polar ends of a spectrum. What I mean by this is that Sam's behaviour is such that either everyone that knows them dislikes them and either shows their intolerance or tolerates Sam on behalf of Chris or, on the other hand, Sam might be the most charming and charismatic person around other people.

The abuser often tells the abused person that no one would believe the fact that they were suffering from domestic violence and abuse. Why? Because the abuser wants the abused person to remain silent, and remain in a relationship with them. Sam might

279

also say to Chris that no one in authority would help or believe them either. This might be actually backed up and reinforced by Chris seeking help from a person in authority, such as the police, a health practitioner, a council official, teacher, doctor etc., and not feeling as if they have been listened to, or been believed. Chris might therefore withdraw and not seek help again, or Chris might have gone to a relative, friend, colleague who also knows Sam and been told by that person that Sam couldn't possibly have been violent or abusive to Chris, and that Chris either must be mistaken, prone to exaggeration, or must have done something to provoke or wind up Sam, or in fact must be spreading malicious rumours about Sam to get Sam in trouble.

So by you telling Chris that you believe what they have just told you, whether it is comprehensible or not, will be extremely important to Chris, to reaffirm that someone they know – you – believes them and is taking them seriously.

4.   Offer them support

When you first hear that someone like Chris has suffered, or is still experiencing, domestic violence and abuse, it might be difficult at first to know what to do. You may have lots of questions rushing around in your mind that you want to ask Chris. But an important thing is to be there to support them.

That support can take a number of forms, such as practical support by helping them write the safety plan, looking after a suitcase or bag containing important documents/items for them, and being there to listen to them whether in person or on the telephone.

The thing to remember is, are you on the same page as Chris when it comes to support? What I mean by this is that we all may be similar to each other on a number of factors and levels, but we can also be different also.

We all come with our own unique different experiences, morals, values and beliefs; our language and terminology may also vary a great deal from a cultural perspective, as well as a geographical perspective (both on an external and internal basis within our designated countries around the world). Therefore, when you offer or provide support, is it support as you know it, or is it the support Chris needs?

One way of being clear about this is by asking Chris what support they actually need, do not assume. The trouble with the term `assume` is that it makes an `ass` out of `u` and `me`, and that we can inadvertently be so far off the mark that we are not being supportive or helpful at all.

5.   Do not lay blame

A common theme with those that are or have been abused is that they are always blamed for everything, whether something is their fault or not in the abusers' mind.

So for example, Sam might say to Chris that they were only shouting at Chris because Chris was winding Sam up or was pushing Sam's buttons. Sam might say that they lashed out at Chris as they had no other choice, that if Chris hadn't done or said the things that they had, then Sam might not have got angry and lashed out. Therefore the violence only happened because of Chris.

Another example of blame is for Sam to say that Chris had been flirting with a third party and the domestic violence and abusive incident only occurred, not because of jealousy, but out of the love Sam has for Chris and anyone else in Sam's position would have done the same.

Children are often blamed for taking the attention and love away from the abuser, so Sam might say that they never wanted children anyway, that it was Chris's fault, and that the children are Chris's responsibility; if the children do anything to upset/annoy or wind up Sam, then it will in Sam's eyes be Chris's fault. Therefore if Sam shouts or chastises the children, the ultimate blame will lay with Chris.

In reality, Sam is responsible for their thoughts, feelings, action and behaviours. No one else is to blame, least of all the Children or Chris.

Even if Sam is frustrated, upset, annoyed or angry, Sam has, if not on their own, but with the help of professional people, the ability to control their reaction to a particular situation. Unfortunately though, Sam will blame Chris for life itself, the world and the universe, so Chris will be used to being blamed and taking the blame for everything.

It is therefore important for you to not blame Chris, and for you to refrain from saying things like: "you must have brought this on yourself," or "you must have done something to provoke Sam," or comments like, "if Sam is violent and abusive, then you are putting the children at risk." Comments like these are not going to help anyone, least of all Chris.

If children are within a household where there is violence and abuse, they are often, both directly and indirectly, involved in the violence and abuse; I mean that if children are in the same room where the violence and abuse is happening, they will not only see the violence and abuse, but will also hear it and will also sense the tension and atmosphere; regardless of the children's ages, there will be some effect and impact on those children. If children are in another room, or upstairs when the violence and abuse is happening, then they might not see it, but they will hear the incident occurring, they will also be scared and frightened for not only their safety but for the ones they love; regardless of the children's ages, the violence and abuse will have some level of impact.

One thing that I have heard numerous times over the years is parents/Carers/guardians saying that the violence and abuse doesn't affect the children. Well it does affect the children on differing levels and scales, and this is often a major deciding factor for the non-abusive parent to leave the relationship, when they realise that their children are and have been affected.

Safety is always paramount and must be the primary concern, but try not to lay blame.

6.   Do not judge them

Society often judges individuals for staying in a domestic violence and abusive relationship, because often most individuals do not understand what domestic violence and abuse is and have no, or limited, awareness of the complexities involved with domestic violence and abuse.

I have heard more times than I wish to remember people saying: *"if it was that bad, the victim would have left"* or *"they must have come from a broken home themselves."* Again, ignorance is often bliss for some people.

Individuals who find themselves within a domestic violence situation come from all walks of life, they can be of any:

- Age
- Background
- Class
- Culture
- Education
- Ethnicity
- Gender
- Location
- Mobility
- Race
- Religion
- Sexuality
- Status
- Spirituality
- Weight

Etc.

So in effect, domestic violence can and does happen to anyone; yes, there are a range of different complexities and aggravating factors, such as alcohol, drugs, money worries, environment, stress, work pressures or lack of work pressures, family pressure, beliefs, values, role models, peer pressure, messages we get from society - so each incident of domestic violence and abuse will have a number of differences and a number of similarities.

Therefore it is important:

1. To listen;
2. To refrain from blaming individuals; and
3. To not judge others.

A Chinese proverb that I have heard in the past, which has always remained with me, is: "judge no man until you have walked two moons in his moccasins."

7.   Avoid Saying

Some people have a habit in life of speaking before thinking, and as a result of this cause unnecessary offense and upset whether they mean it or not.

Individuals that have experienced, or are still experiencing, domestic violence and abuse will have an increased sense of awareness and sensitivity to that which is happening around them, and things that are being said also.

They often have this heightened sense, in order to be able to assess how to manage/handle/deal with or react to the abuser, in

286

order to be able to `survive` and continue to function through daily life (not all are able to function without the use of coping mechanisms, which can rebound and become addictions).

Often the abused individual does what they can, with the awareness and life skills that they have at that particular time and under the circumstances that they find themselves in.

Therefore, comments like the following 3 <u>don't</u> help:

1. *"If I were you, I would have left Sam years ago," or "I would have left the minute Sam raised a hand to me."*

2. *"I understand what you are going through, Joe or Jane Bloggs went through the same thing."*

3. *"It cannot be that bad or you wouldn't still be there," or "everyone has arguments."*

So if we look further at the comments in the previous 3 points:

1. By saying things like these, inadvertently you will make Chris feel much worse than Chris feels already, if that is at all possible, and I am sure that you would not intentionally want to hurt Chris.

2.   No one can 'understand' what another person experiences through domestic violence and abuse, even if the other person has experienced domestic violence and abuse themselves, as each specific experience will be different because of the individual's unique factors relating to them. What another person can do however is empathise with someone like Chris and take into consideration all of the 7 Key Tips above in order to make a difference.

3.   Individuals like Chris minimise the violence and abuse in order to manage, deal with and cope. Therefore they will play down rather than exaggerate. By making comments like point 3 above, you will only be reinforcing that Chris should stay in the relationships and work with whatever happens as it is 'normal'.

Appendix 3

Breaking the Cycle – 'Escaping Victimhood'

I am sure, like me, you have heard of 'The Secret' or 'The Law of Attraction', where they highlight that if you want to be successful then you should surround yourself with successful people; if you want an abundance of wealth then train your mind that you already have that wealth and it will follow.

You may have reservations around these statements, as I have had throughout my life.

It doesn't just work with attracting positive things into my life; unfortunately it works with negative and harmful things, so I needed to work on changing my thought processes.

Thinking of it in terms of my own life, I thought to myself, why do I always end up being a 'victim'? The answer was right in front of me: because I felt like a victim, I was focusing on the fact other people would take advantage and manipulate situations where I would end up losing out and then ultimately I would feel like and become a 'victim'.

I am not advocating or suggesting that I brought things on myself, because there are always individuals out there who are ready and do take advantage in a deceptive and controlling way. There are also individuals out there that work on the basis of using power and control to manipulate, bully, intimidate and are abusive to others and I cannot change those individuals, and neither can you, and yet we use up a lot of our time trying to change them, or giving them the benefit of the doubt.

However, I can address what is within my control, such as my reactions to situations or events.

I changed my mindset from the present tense of *being* a victim to the past tense of *having been* a victim.

Having previously been a victim of domestic violence, I know that I couldn't change my ex partner's behaviour and that perhaps, at a number of stages during our relationship, I didn't have the strength or courage to leave; I thought it was my fault, that they were behaving in that way because of me, my self-esteem disappeared and my confidence fell, therefore I believed it was my fault. In reality, it wasn't my fault at all, and the evidence was there if I had only been in a position to see it at the time, there was violence in their family, their past relationships had been volatile and violence had been prevalent and they had a Jekyll and Hyde personality.

What was within my control was changing any negative self-talk into positive self-talk – albeit I didn't realise that at the time during the relationship.

Again, during situations in other environments when confronted by difficult individuals, although my conscious mind recognised the fact that these individuals were difficult with everyone, my unconscious mind was screaming out thoughts such as: "it always happens to you" or "here we go again" or "what are you doing to bring this on?"

Of course, other people's behaviour was outside of my control, but by thinking "why me?", then actually, if the law of attraction works, then I was attracting that behaviour towards me, by thinking "This always happens to me" and then it did always happen to me!

I therefore needed to change the way I thought about things and reframe the words that I used. Not as easy as it sounds, always having been someone who, if nineteen positive things were said about me and only one negative thing, I actually would focus on the one negative thing, but I am not unique in that, as many of you may well be the same.

In the past, writing down a list of positive and negative things in my life, or about me, has helped me to visualise and absorb some of the positivity:

Positive Characteristics	Negative Characteristics
Good Listener	Shy
Non Judgmental	Elusive
Caring	Distant
Thoughtful	Withdrawn
Passionate	Quiet
Loving	
Approachable	
Considerate	
Practical	
Reliable	

The table indicates that the positive characteristics outweigh the negative but also, on closer reflection when I broke down the negative ones, they all came about due to other people's behaviour in my life and my reaction to their behaviour.

I had a responsibility in letting someone's behaviour impact on my life for many years – the responsibility was not their behaviour, but my reaction to it.

Whilst at school and throughout my childhood, I was never distant, withdrawn or elusive, I was the practical joker, always having a good laugh; I played sports and was outgoing in that respect. I may have been on occasion mistaken for being a little shy, but that was actually due to the fact that I was more reflective as a person, I liked to weigh things up and preferred to let things register in my brain before answering or coming back on something.

The withdrawn and distant labels came from the environments that I was in and I felt exposed and vulnerable; these labels then resurfaced within a controlling and manipulative relationship. I had never experienced the emotions associated with bullying or domestic violence in my childhood, therefore I didn't know how to deal with or cope with them, so rather than think at the time that these issues were down to the bully or perpetrator, I internalised the emotions, which therefore impacted on my health and my emotional wellbeing.

In order to cope, I put up a barrier around me, as in to defend myself from any hurt or pain, gaining me the labels of withdrawn, distant or cold. For me though, it was a way to preserve my inner feelings, my inner self from being wounded further.

What I have learnt over the years though, is that whilst the barrier is effective then all well and good, but once you let someone get close to you and they are able to penetrate the barrier, the feelings and emotions are immense, and if that relationship, whether an intimate, close friendship or work based relationship breaks down, then the scars from the past are opened up a little more and the wounds are liable to go deeper, in essence compounding things further.

I recognised the fact that if I just blocked out, or 'parked' the emotions and feelings, then they didn't go away, they just stayed there and waited for an ideal opportunity to resurface and that such opportunity was often when I felt vulnerable or my confidence was at a low ebb, therefore it wasn't the best time for other unresolved feelings or emotions to have re-entered my life.

I therefore took a different approach of dealing with my emotions or feelings. So learning to reflect on what was going on, how was I feeling, what was I experiencing, what was I thinking, for example: If I felt sad, I would look at what physical signs I was showing, what had happened to make me feel sad, was the reason because of something that was within my control or outside of it, was there something that I could have done to rectify the situation? If yes, then could I do something, if no then I would look at my reactions to the event or situation.

My reaction to something is what I have within my control. I have the ability with practice to change my thoughts, feelings and my actions.

The aim is to move away from the thoughts of what you <u>don't</u> want and to move towards thoughts of what you <u>do</u> want.

What I DON'T Want	What I DO Want
To feel trapped	To have my freedom
To be bullied	To be confident
To feel worthless	To be happy
To be sad	To be self-assured
To be unhappy	To feel valued
To feel like giving up	To be respected
To have no confidence	To follow my dreams
To be a victim	To be successful
To be controlled	To be in control of my destiny
To feel negativity	To have positive thoughts

From the previous table, we then need to reflect on the words and to break down what each of these means to us, and to then look at what steps we can take to achieve these changes:

What DO I Want?	What that will look like	What I need to do
To have my freedom	Do things I want to do	Do more things for myself
To be confident	Not worry what others say	Believe in myself
To be happy	Not feeling sad all the while	Do things that make me happy

When we are able to shift and move our mindset away from being a victim, we can then truly begin the healing process of reclaiming our inner self.

Changing our mindset isn't easy and will take practice and time to master, but what you can do is look at some of the negative things you say about yourself and look at how you could possibly reframe that thought or statement in a more positive way, for example:

I find it difficult to make new friends.

If you find it difficult to make new friends, and that is what you are telling yourself, then as the law of attraction suggests it will be difficult to make new friends, as you are reinforcing that difficulty. A way of perhaps reframing this might be:

I am open to the opportunities of making new friends.

296

Changing negative thoughts requires practice, as we have throughout our lives been told that we cannot do things because of a variety of reasons: because of our background, our gender, our age, ethnicity, sexuality, our social status, or intellect... but we have an option, a choice to reframe negative thoughts into positive ones.... in order to escape victimhood and move forward, we first need to get out of our own way.

Try reframing some of your negative self-talk into positive self-talk.

Negative Self Talk	Positive Self Talk
I am no good at anything	I am intelligent, practical and capable
I feel overweight and unattractive	I am beautiful both inside and out
I don't fit in	I love myself for my uniqueness and for being me

You may also find using `Affirmations` beneficial to you.

When I was in a difficult place after a relationship breakdown, I listened to an audio book that talked about using positive statements (Affirmations) over and over again in order for the statement to sink into your unconscious mind, which in turn would then work at achieving those positive statements.

I was sceptical at first, but I thought that, as I was feeling pretty low, it wouldn't harm to give it a go. So I began to think about what I wanted in the 'here and now' and for the future, so these are some of the statements (affirmations) that I wrote down:

1. I am a happy and confident person.
2. I love and value myself as an individual.
3. I am beautiful both inside and out.
4. I can achieve anything I set my mind to.
5. I am happy with my weight and lifestyle.
6. I am a size ten and content.
7. Others find what I say interesting and valuable.
8. I am content with my own company.

I would continually say these affirmations over and over for about an hour each night before I went to bed and when I awoke each morning. I remember continuing with this routine for about two to three months and what I noticed was that my whole mindset had changed. I believed in all eight affirmations and they seemed to be working, including having lost three stone in weight without working out at the gym, or without going on a crash course diet.

So there seemed to be an element of truth in the 'Law of Attraction', in 'Negative and Positive Self Talk' and in 'Affirmations'. Of course, I'm no different to anyone else, because I do things for a while and then I slip back into a routine of doing nothing.

One thing that is abundantly clear though, is that in order to sustain things, we must continue to work at it, it needs to be a complete lifestyle change within our mindset, we must continue to attract what we do want in our lives, and not what we don't want... i.e. by saying "I don't want to be poor," will in effect attract me to being poor, whereas if I say "I do want to be rich," I will attract riches. It's not that a bag of money will drop down from the sky, when I say 'think it and it will come to you', I mean subconsciously you will be working on things, however small, every single day to achieve this aim.

The mind is continuously working 24/7 and we need to be aware of both our conscious and unconscious processes. What we think consciously our unconscious will set about working towards, therefore we need to reframe how we think for the appropriate results, and in order to move from victimhood to freedom for our inner self, we need to stop thinking of ourselves as a victim and see ourselves as being the creator of our own destiny and moving towards our hopes, dreams and goals.

Acknowledgements

I would like to thank all those who have played a part in my journey to date: my family, especially my mum, dad, sister and brother-in-law, your unwavering support and love throughout the years have helped me through some very dark and difficult times and it is difficult to express in words the thanks and appreciation I owe you all.

To my Nan, you are never far from my thoughts; although treasured, eighteen years never seem like enough.

To my close friends, my colleagues within the 'police family' and my colleagues in the wider field of domestic violence and relationship difficulties, your support and friendships have been invaluable to me over the years.

To Chris Bainbridge, thank you for your guidance and support over many years. Your determination and hard work set the benchmark for the work surrounding domestic violence within Essex Police. You have been and continue to be my role model and mentor, and it is a real privilege and honour to know you and call you my friend.

To all the amazing, strong and brave victims of domestic violence that I have met over the last few decades, you keep my passion alive and motivate me to continue to make a difference.

To my wonderful and supportive partner who is my soul mate, who keeps inspiring me to live out my dreams and be who I want to be and who continues to love me in the way I deserve to be loved.

To 'My Rock', without whom I wouldn't be here today. You are always in my heart.

2570124R00181

Printed in Germany
by Amazon Distribution
GmbH, Leipzig